Patricia Lehman

Cairn Terriers

Everything about Purchase, Care, Nutrition, Grooming, Behavior, and Training

Filled with Full-color Photographs
Illustrations by Pam Tanzey

BARRON'S

2CONTENTS

UNDERSTANDING YOUR CAIRN TERRIER

Scotland's Earth Dogs

Recognized as one of Scotland's earliest working dogs, the Cairn Terrier originated on the heather-covered hills of the northwest Highlands and the rugged and remote Isle of Skye in the Hebrides. Dogs that closely resembled the Cairn have been identified as a distinct group on the misty isle for more than two hundred years. Called Scotch or Highland Terriers, Skye or Skye Otter Terriers, Todhunters (tod is a Scottish word for fox), or even Fox Terriers, these forerunners of the present-day Cairn Terrier quickly gained a reputation for courage and determination.

Bred solely for their ability to do the job required of them rather than physical appearance or type, Scotland's native earth dogs played a key role in the lives of the men who worked them. Along the country's northwestern shores—a desolate region known for its long coastline edged with rocky cliffs—wildlife abounded, and small animals sought refuge within the crevices of enormous boulders. It was also a custom among early inhabitants to assemble piles of

Its quick mind, combined with its eagerness to please, enables the Cairn to readily master tricks.

stones, or *cairns*, for use as grave markers, property boundaries, and landmarks. These distinctive sentinels, inert to the casual observer, teemed with secret life as a variety of small mammals nestled into their hiding places.

Hunters who lived in isolated areas that bordered the Atlantic Ocean used their small, shaggy-haired terriers to rout otters and badgers—valued for their skins—from their shelter in cliffs and cairns. Landowners who raised sheep for the profitable wool trade, headquartered at Inverness, also utilized the dogs to drive out foxes that often killed their lambs. In addition, many outlying districts employed itinerant todhunters, or *brocaires*, who used packs of terriers to rid the countryside of vermin.

Working closely with their masters, and occasionally a hound or two that tracked by scent, these valiant canines followed their quarry into passages so small and twisting that no man could enter. Neither could the stones be moved; the smallest weighed two or three tons. Alone but unafraid, the terrier penetrated the dark corridors in search of its prey. The dog's responsibility was not to kill the animal—or even to engage it in battle—but to flush it from its lair so it could be snared or shot by the keeper. Few terriers retreated without their prizes and many a "game little bit of dogflesh" carried the scars of its efforts.

Scottish lairds and landowners prized their packs of terriers. As early as 1600, James VI of Scotland (James I of England) sang the praises of the "earth dogges" of Argyllshire.

his Waternish terriers solely for their working ability, and preferred a "smart, plucky" mate regardless of its appearance. MacLeod's Drynoch terriers, with their distinctive prick ears, stand behind many of the early British champions. Martin MacKinnon's family, of Kilbride and Kyle, also maintained a notable line, descended from the prized strain established by Farquhar Kelly in the seventeenth century. Although a Scotsman would never part with his best dogs, as the untamed north became more accessible to outsiders, puppies eventually made their way into the homes of admirers. In fact, several individuals who later judged the Cairn Terrier in the show ring recognized the breed as the same type of Highland terrier they had owned as pets during childhood.

The Great Clan Kennels

Nearly every laird possessed his kennel of terriers in mid-nineteenth-century Scotland. Strains developed by the MacLeod, MacDonald, and MacKinnon families, according to early breeding records, figure prominently in the background of the Cairn Terrier. Captain MacLeod, of Drynoch, and Captain MacDonald, of Waternish, were avid sportsmen on the Isle of Skye. MacDonald, who admitted he would wait at the cairns all night for an otter, bred

In the Show Ring

By the 1860s, dog shows had become a popular means of comparing dogs based on their physical characteristics, temperament, and ability to present themselves in the ring. Terriers of Scottish descent initially competed as Scotch Terriers. As shows began to offer more classes, Cairns moved to the Hard-haired Scotch Terrier group, which also included Scottish and West

Manmade rock formations, called cairns, denote the location of graves, property boundaries, and other landmarks.

Highland White Terriers. In fact, the three kinds of terrier came from the same ancestral bloodlines and often appeared in the same litters. At this point, no fixed standards had been drafted and type varied widely among the entries. Judges knew little of the breeds' distinctive points, although each owner insisted that his dogs represented the archetype.

Mrs. Alastair Campbell, an early fancier credited with singlehandedly gaining breed recognition, devised the name, "Short-haired Skye Terrier," because she felt the dogs were the original terriers of the Isle of Skye. Several dogs competed under this title at the Inverness and Crufts shows, in 1909, with blue ribbons going to Fassie and Doran Bhan, respectively. However, the inclusion of the Cairn as a variety of Skye Terrier caused considerable controversy among members of the Skye Terrier Club, who supported the long-haired Skye as the true type. After Mrs. Campbell and another exhibitor entered their Cairns in the class for Skye Terriers, rather than Short-haired Skyes, at the 1910 Crufts show, the matter finally came to a head. The breed club organized a committee to work with the national Kennel Club to resolve the confusion over the dog's name.

The Countess of Aberdeen suggested "Cairn Terrier of Skye," because of the breed's connection to the rocky cairns of northwestern Scotland. Robert Leighton, a prominent dog judge and canine historian, urged the club to accept

the shortened form, Cairn Terrier, which was already in use in the Highlands. In 1910, after they gained approval for the new name, enthusiasts organized the Cairn Terrier Club. The following year, members drew up the official standard and scale of points (see pages 10–11). By the time the first champions, Tibbie of Harris and Gesto, were crowned two years later, the breed was well on its way to popularity. As the threat of World War I darkened Great Britain's skies, dogs from many of the top kennels were exported to other countries, including the United States, Canada, and Australia, where they formed the foundation behind today's outstanding Cairn Terriers.

Known for their courage and determination, Cairn Terriers assisted their masters in routing foxes, badgers, otters, and other small mammals from their hidden dens.

Cairn Terriers in America

Like many of the dogs that traveled across the Atlantic Ocean at the dawn of the twentieth century, some of the earliest Cairn Terriers to arrive in the United States were pets that accompanied owners relocating to America from the British Isles. Although its precise beginning in this country is shrouded in the mists of its ancient homeland, the first identifiable Cairn was a sandy-haired dog with black points, called Sandy Peter out of the West, that entered the AKC's Stud Book in 1913. The breed became the last of Scotland's terriers to gain formal recognition, in 1917, when the Cairn Terrier Club of America (CTCA) was founded. The following year, Greentree Ardsheal Gillie Cam earned the first conformation championship. In 1927, Jinx Ballantrae, owned by well-known actors Kenneth Harlan and Marie

This early postcard depicts a Cairn Terrier (center) with its cousins, the Scottish Terrier and West Highland White Terrier.

Prevost, became the first Cairn to win the coveted Best in Show award. Champion Tidewater Master Gold made history, in 1988, as the first of its breed to win the Terrier Group and compete for Best in Show at the prestigious Westminster Kennel Club dog show. Cairn Terriers continue to excel in the show ring, as well as in Obedience and Performance events.

Canine Companion

"Game as a pebble, lively as a cricket, and all in all a most charming little companion," is how one historian described the Cairn Terrier. This is

From the heather-covered hills of the Scottish Highlands to its new home in America, the Cairn has charmed fanciers with its intelligence, courage, and heart of gold.

a breed in transition. Although vestiges remain of its instincts as a working terrier—independence, courage, and a large-dog attitude—the Cairn has become fully integrated as a member of its human family. Cairns are not one-person dogs, but flourish with the attention that comes from being part of a larger "pack." Their fun-loving and spirited, yet kindhearted, dispositions also make them wonderful playmates for children. Whether engaging in a rough-and-tumble game or offering a furry shoulder to cry on, a Cairn has a remarkable ability to sense a youngster's mood and adjust its behavior accordingly. Of course, close supervision of children and pets is essential to maintain a harmonious relationship. Parents must teach youngsters that dogs are not playthings, but living creatures that require patience, understanding, and kindness in order to thrive.

However, despite their need for companionship, Cairns are not typical lap dogs. Young dogs, in particular, prefer to explore their newfound domains rather than rest quietly for any length of time. This alertness to their surroundings, along with their range of vocalizations, makes them natural watchdogs. Different tones and pitches in barking mean different things, according to one owner, such as the approach of a mail carrier, stray dog, or trespassing squirrel. Cairns are not quarrelsome with other animals, but will stand their ground when the situation demands confidence.

Perhaps because of their close association with humans—even when they shared the crofter's hearth and home in earlier times—Cairns are sensitive, eager to please, and highly intelligent. They not only respond to verbal commands and corrections, but also to their owners' body language. Physical discipline is rarely necessary, once you've seen the look of hurt in a Cairn's eyes that a mere reprimand can bring. This uncommon ability to identify nonverbal signals applies to owners, as well. Devotees have discovered that they can interpret their dogs' emotions by watching their actions—especially the carriage of their expressive, upright ears.

Cairns may have difficulty achieving top scores in obedience trials because of their creative and amusing antics, but the dogs are highly intelligent and capable of learning almost any feat their owners care to teach them. "The more time a person spends with a Cairn Terrier, the more personality and intelligence it will display," claims longtime breeder and canine author, Betty E. Marcum. She adds, "I have seen Cairns do uncanny things that definitely bespeak greater intelligence than mankind attributes to 'dumb' animals."

These qualities, and many others, have led owners to unanimously avow: After you've owned a Cairn Terrier with the true temperament of the breed, you'll never choose another dog.

The Breed Standard

To preserve the characteristics of Scotland's original working terriers, the first breed standard adopted by the Cairn Terrier Club of America, in 1917, closely followed the one approved six years earlier by The Kennel Club of Great Britain. The current standard, listed below, was approved by the Cairn Terrier Club of America on May 10, 1938.

General Appearance—That of an active, game, hardy, small working terrier of the short-legged class; very free in its movements, strongly but not heavily built, standing well forward on its forelegs, deep in the ribs, well coupled with strong hindquarters and presenting a well-proportioned build with a medium length of back, having a hard, weather-resisting coat; head shorter and wider than any other terrier and well furnished with hair giving a general foxy expression.

Head—*Skull*—Broad in proportion to length with a decided stop and well furnished with hair on the top of the head, which may be somewhat softer than the body coat. *Muzzle*—Strong but not too long or heavy. *Teeth*—Large, mouth neither overshot nor undershot. *Nose*—Black. *Eyes*—Set wide apart, rather sunken, with shaggy eyebrows, medium in size, hazel or dark hazel in color, depending on body color, with a keen terrier expression. *Ears*—Small, pointed, well carried erectly, set wide apart on the side of the head. Free from long hairs.

Tail—In proportion to head, well furnished with hair but not feathery. Carried gaily but must not curl over back. Set on at back level.

Body—Well-muscled, strong, active body with well-sprung, deep ribs, coupled to strong hindquarters, with a level back of medium length, giving an impression of strength and activity without heaviness.

Shoulders, Legs, and Feet—A sloping shoulder, medium length of leg, good but not too heavy bone; forelegs should not be out at elbows, and be perfectly straight, but forefeet may be slightly turned out. Forefeet larger than hind feet. Legs must be covered with hard hair. Pads should be thick and strong and dog should stand well up on its feet.

Coat—Hard and weather-resistant. Must be double-coated with profuse harsh outer coat and short, soft, close furry undercoat.

Color—May be of any color except white. Dark ears, muzzle and tail tip are desirable.

Ideal Size—Involves the weight, the height at the withers and the length of body. Weight for bitches, 13 pounds; for dogs, 14 pounds. Height at the withers — bitches, 9½ inches; dogs, 10 inches. Length of body from 14¼ to 15 inches from the front of the chest to back of hindquarters. The dog must be of balanced proportions and appear neither leggy nor too low to ground; and neither too short nor too long in body. Weight and measurements are for matured dogs at two years of age. Older dogs may weigh slightly in excess and growing dogs may be under these weights and measurements.

Condition—Dogs should be shown in good hard flesh, well muscled and neither too fat nor too thin. Should be in full good coat with plenty of head furnishings, be clean, combed, brushed and tidied up on ears, tail, feet, and general outline. Should move freely and easily on a loose lead, should not cringe on being handled, should stand up on their toes and show with marked terrier characteristics.

FAULTS

1. *Skull*—Too narrow in skull.

2. *Muzzle*—Too long and heavy a foreface; mouth overshot or undershot.

3. *Eyes*—Too large, prominent, yellow, and ringed are all objectionable.

4. *Ears*—Too large, round at points, set too close together, set too high on the head; heavily covered with hair.

5. *Legs and Feet*—Too light or too heavy bone. Crooked forelegs or out at elbow. Thin, ferrety feet; feet let down on the heel or too open and spread. Too high or too low on the leg.

6. *Body*—Too short back and compact a body, hampering quickness of movement and turning ability. Too long, weedy and snaky a body, giving an impression of weakness. Tail set on too low. Back not level.

7. *Coat*—Open coats, blousy coats, too short or dead coats, lack of sufficient undercoat, lack of head furnishings, lack of hard hair on the legs. Silkiness or curliness. A slight wave permissible.

8. *Nose*—Flesh or light-colored nose.

9. *Color*—White on chest, feet, or other parts of body.

CONSIDERATIONS BEFORE YOU BUY

When a scruffy Cairn Terrier joined the Ricardo family after following Little Ricky home one day, viewers of the popular *I Love Lucy* television series reveled as the puppy's mischief rivaled that of his red-haired mistress. Problems with neighbors and frequent disappearances led to obedience school, where reluctant Fred finally earned his diploma. Although Hollywood productions have promoted spur-of-the-moment pet ownership on TV, as well as in the movies, the decision to acquire a Cairn Terrier requires considerable thought, study, and personal reflection.

Dog Ownership

Before you purchase a Cairn, which can live 15 or more years with proper attention, it's important to think not only about the benefits but also the obligations involved in owning a dog. To help you decide whether a Cairn, or any breed, is right for you, ask yourself the following questions:

Why Do I Want a Dog?

People own Cairns for reasons as diverse as the dogs themselves: the challenge of compet-

This adventurous youngster explores a backyard wood pile with its adult companion.

ing in dog shows, the rewards of obedience training, the excitement of participating in performance events, the satisfaction of breeding champion-caliber animals, and, most of all, the enjoyment that comes from sharing a home with a loving canine companion. Unfortunately, some individuals choose dogs for the wrong reasons. Owners concerned with an image, for instance, often acquire certain breeds as status symbols, without regard to their suitability as family pets. Others fall victim to unscrupulous sellers who demand large sums for traits that, in reality, are considered faults or disqualifications. People also purchase dogs to teach responsibility to their children. Although the bond between a child and dog is one of the strongest of all youthful relationships, keep in mind that most tasks related to an animal's care eventually fall on the parents. Many Cairn breeders are reluctant to sell to homes with children younger than seven or eight, unless assured that adults will supervise the rearing of the puppy. Owning a dog is not a whim, but a lifelong commitment that should be entered into only if you're willing to give as much to the relationship as does your Cairn Terrier.

Is My Lifestyle Compatible With Dog Ownership?

Another consideration is whether a dog fits into your lifestyle. As one of the smaller terriers, standing about 10 inches at the shoulders, Cairns readily adapt to country estates, suburban dwellings, or downtown apartments. In fact, one of the most successful kennels of the 1920s and 1930s began in an apartment on Park Avenue in New York City. However, because Cairns are quite active and need to work off their excess energy, make certain you can take your dog for at least two walks each day. Also, check your lease before you bring home a puppy to ensure that your landlord allows dogs. If you own a home, a fenced-in backyard provides adequate space for exercise. Cairns should not be left alone for long periods, though, because they tend to become destructive diggers. The breed's hunting instincts remain strong, as well. Can you tolerate a dog that goes after small prey—even showing off its "kill" to owners?

Assess your schedule before you adopt a Cairn. Do you work long or irregular hours? Have an active social life or travel frequently? Puppies, in particular, demand a constant routine. You must make a commitment to exercise and interact with the dog, feed at planned intervals, and groom consistently. Your Cairn should not go without

dinner just because you have to work late. If you travel, you'll need to make arrangements with a reliable pet sitter or boarding kennel.

Do you have other pets? If you already own one or more dogs, discuss with the breeder whether a puppy is likely to get along with adult dogs. Choose a puppy of the opposite sex to your dog and have both animals neutered. Females tend to bicker among themselves as often as do males. If you have a cat, look for a puppy that has been socialized with cats. Cairns generally are not suitable for homes with exotic pets, such as mice, gerbils, or hamsters, because the terriers might mistake them for prey.

Do I Have Time to Housebreak, Socialize, and Train a Dog?

It's vital to know whether your routine allows sufficient time for all facets of training before you add a dog to your household. Can you take your Cairn for walks at lunchtime? Is someone available during the day to let out a puppy? Although grown dogs may be able to wait several hours to relieve themselves, puppies cannot be confined for more than two hours at a time. Puppies need adequate socialization, as well, so they can learn how to behave around strangers, children, and other animals. This entails exposing your Cairn to a variety of situations (after it's been fully inoculated against infectious diseases), such as riding in the car, walking in public places, visiting friends, and interacting with other pets. Attending puppy

Puppy kindergarten classes, which emphasize fundamental training rather than formal obedience, help young dogs develop valuable social skills.

kindergarten classes, given by a kennel club or community organization, is an ideal way to help a young dog develop self-confidence as well as self-control. Be sure to allot time to work on the basic commands—come, sit, down, stay, and heel—and, if possible, to participate in formal obedience classes with your Cairn.

Am I Prepared for the Financial Responsibilities of Owning a Dog?

The price of a Cairn, which ranges from $500 to $800 for a pet quality puppy, is only the beginning of your expenses. Before you bring your puppy home, you'll need a crate, collar, leash, bedding, bowls, food, toys, and grooming supplies. You'll also want to invest in a training manual and veterinary reference. Your puppy will need a checkup by a veterinarian within 48 to 72 hours, a series of inoculations, and neutering by six months of age. Figure in the cost of annual examinations and vaccinations, dental care, medications, tests, and other procedures. Additional outlays include food, professional grooming, obedience classes, and boarding when you travel.

Do I Understand, and Am I Willing to Obey, My Community's Dog Laws?

A significant aspect of responsible dog ownership is the willingness to comply with local regulations, such as keeping your dog on a leash and under control at all times, cleaning up after your pet in public places, obtaining rabies inoculations according to your state's requirements, and purchasing yearly dog licenses. Most communities also have rules against excessive barking (especially at night), roaming dogs, and neglect or abuse. Some areas have imposed restrictions on the number of dogs permitted in a household, while others regulate, or even prohibit, breeding kennels. Before you purchase a Cairn Terrier, make certain you're familiar with your town's dog-related ordinances.

Puppy or Adult?

With its winsome expression, bright eyes, ragamuffin coat, and wagging tail, a Cairn Terrier's appeal is nearly impossible to resist. If you're thinking of adding a Cairn to your household, one of the first decisions you'll have to make is whether to choose a puppy, an adolescent, or a full-grown dog. Many owners prefer a puppy because they want to participate in all aspects of raising a dog, especially if it's their first experience with a pet. Young animals willingly accept training and bad habits have not yet become established. Puppies also are eager to bond with their families and readily adjust to new routines. Caring for a puppy is delightful for children as well, because they can take an active part in training and see how the dog grows and develops. However, puppies are not without potential problems. Like other terriers, Cairns are high-spirited, energetic, and playful. Some take up to two years to settle down, so don't expect a lap dog until well into its adulthood. Puppies also require attention and supervision, even when you have other priorities for your time.

Because of these factors, an older puppy or adult dog might be the best choice for your family. Cairns that are already housebroken and obedience trained make excellent choices for active households or owners who want immediate companions. Mature dogs also are ideal for senior citizens who might lack the stamina for long walks or prefer more sedate pets.

Male or Female?

Because males and females are similar in appearance, size, and personality, either would make a fine pet. Males are usually more alert and active than females, and some owners consider them more possessive about their territorial boundaries. With their distinctive barks and yaps that announce the arrival of visitors, strangers, or other animals, they make excellent watch dogs. Although Cairns won't start neighborhood fights, few will back down if challenged. Males also tend to display greater intelligence and affection than females, according to several owners who unanimously used the term, "sweet," to describe their Cairns.

Females, on the other hand, are a bit more "catlike" and independent than males. Often, they rule other dogs in the household until one of them establishes the *alpha*, or top-dog, position. However, many people characterize them as loving, affectionate, outgoing, and friendly. They especially enjoy the company of children, greeting them with wet tongues and wagging tails. Females are generally easier to train than males, and display fewer undesirable behaviors.

Temperament Comes First

When deciding whether to purchase a male or female, keep an open mind and don't rule out a Cairn that fits your requirements in every other way. The most important factor in selecting any pet is temperament. Try to view each dog as an individual, instead of assigning traits based on gender. Most characteristics—good and bad—are found in both sexes. Neutering males before six months of age often counteracts problems such as marking territory and roaming. In females, it eliminates estrous cycles and unwanted pregnancies. Keep in mind that the environment in which a puppy is raised greatly affects its personality. Likewise, it's vital to continue the breeder's efforts by socializing and training your Cairn Terrier.

Show Quality or Pet Quality?

When breeders interact with their litters, they often notice subtle variations among puppies that are difficult for buyers to distinguish. Characteristics such as head shape, tail set, length of back, and overall balance become apparent within the first few weeks. So, too, do the puppies' personalities—their enthusiasm or indifference, friendliness or shyness. Each breed has an official written standard that describes the ideal specimen. Although it's impossible to guarantee that a puppy will become a champion before it sets a paw in the ring, breeders can usually predict a dog's potential for success based on how closely it conforms to the standard.

If you're a novice seeking a show-quality Cairn Terrier, expect the breeder to question you about your experience with dogs. What breeds are you familiar with? Have you worked with terriers

Reflecting the muted shades of the mist-shrouded Hebrides, this group includes silver, charcoal, and wheaten coat colors.

before? Have you finished a champion? If you think competing might be fun for you and your family, make certain everyone is committed to the training, specialized grooming, extensive travel, and high entry fees associated with gaining a title. Most handlers travel every weekend, regardless of weather, distance, and accommodations, to show sites across the country.

You may need to provide a reference from a local kennel club before a breeder will sell you a quality Cairn. Don't expect the breeder's most promising puppy, even if you can afford to pay $800 to $1,500, until you have proven you're serious about showing dogs. Novices often acquire Cairns on co-ownership agreements, with stipulations about how and when they will show the animals. Others select older puppies or adults as their first show dogs.

By far, the majority of Cairns go to pet homes where they take blue ribbons as "champions of hearts."

Color Choices

Any coat color, except white, is permissible for Cairn Terriers. This includes cream, wheaten, red and red wheaten, silver and silver wheaten, and varying shades of gray. Darker points on the ears, muzzle, and tail tip are highly desirable. A brindle pattern—bands of black pigment on a lighter background—also is found in the breed. In fact, an early fancier identified 24 shades or mixtures in a study conducted during the 1930s. However, the difficulty in selecting a puppy is because of not only the array of possible choices, but also the tendency of the coat to change color throughout the dog's lifetime. Cream or wheaten puppies may become silver, silver brindle, or dark gray; silvers may become golden; reds may become red brindle or dark gray.

Locating Your Cairn Terrier

Your Cairn will be part of your family for many years to come, so it's important to purchase a quality dog from a responsible breeder. Such breeders not only are concerned with producing animals that are physically and mentally sound, but also are committed to improving the breed. Responsible breeders plan each litter to make certain they bring together the best possible mates. They study hereditary diseases that are known to occur and take steps to screen their bloodlines for potential problems. Breeders who truly care about Cairns stand behind every dog they sell throughout its lifetime. They carefully screen buyers to determine whether the breed will meet their expectations, and insist on taking back dogs that owners no longer can keep. By their willingness to answer questions and assist with problems, breeders play a vital part in educating the next generation of fanciers.

The Parent Club

To begin your search for that perfect Cairn, contact the parent club for a list of member breeders. If you're considering an adult dog, ask for the name and telephone number of the rescue committee chairperson. Request a copy of the brochure, *Meet the Cairn Terrier*, which you also may download from the club's Web site. (See Information, page 90.) Another place to find conscientious breeders is at a dog show—either an all-breed event or, better yet, a regional specialty show featuring only Cairns. The premier competition for terriers of all kinds is the Montgomery County Kennel Club dog show, held each year in Ambler, Pennsylvania. It's always a good idea to view adult dogs, as well as puppies, before settling on a particular breed. Be sure to purchase the show catalog, which includes the names and addresses of participating exhibitors. Watch the Cairns that compete in the Obedience ring, too. (Although Montgomery does not offer Obedience, most shows do.) Kennels that produce trainable dogs are good choices for owners looking for intelligent pets. Other sources for referrals are veterinarians, groomers, training instructors, and boarding kennels. Many local dog clubs know reliable breeders, and some offer referral services by telephone.

Visiting the Breeder

After you have narrowed your list of possible kennels, contact the breeders to find out whether they have any Cairns that might meet your requirements for age, sex, temperament, and overall quality. Make an appointment to visit the breeder and see the adult dogs before you view the puppies. Are they in good condition— clean, groomed, and well fed? Friendly, outgoing, and eager to greet visitors? The kind of dogs you hope your puppy will take after when it grows up? Never buy from a kennel where the adults have temperament problems or are poorly maintained. Although you may sympathize with animals raised in such surroundings, you'll stand a better chance of closing down a puppy mill by refusing to benefit the owner and contacting the local humane association.

Selecting the Right Dog

Perhaps the most difficult aspect of acquiring a Cairn is choosing your favorite from a group of robust terriers. If you have decided on a puppy, schedule your visit to the breeder for a time when the puppies are likely to be active and alert. Usually, this is an hour or two before a meal. During the visit—and you may want to see them more than once before you make your decision—watch how they interact with their littermates and mother, as well as with you alone. Cairns should be happy, lively, playful, and interested in their surroundings. Often, a puppy will stand out as the cutest, nicest, or most affectionate. However, the one that immediately runs to greet you also may be the most dominant puppy in the litter. These "live wires" usually do best in homes with experienced terrier fanciers; average owners sometimes have trouble controlling them. Don't overlook the serious youngster, which often blooms when it becomes the chief dog in its new household. Steer clear of overly timid, trembling, hyperactive, or snappy puppies. Be cautious in choosing the runt of the litter as well, because a small puppy may have health problems that are not yet apparent. If you encounter someone trying to sell poorly bred Cairns, leave and look for a breeder who raises his or her dogs with the care they deserve.

After you have found a puppy you like, inspect it carefully from head to tail. Are the eyes clear and bright, with no discharge or cloudiness? The ears clean and odor free? The nose moist and cool? If the puppy teeth are in, do they meet in the correct bite? Be wary of any puppy that wheezes, sneezes, coughs, or vomits. These may be temporary problems, but they could signal a more serious illness. Notice the condition of the coat. Is it clean, shiny, and thick? Is the skin healthy, with no crusty patches or sores? A dry, dull coat, or one with bald spots, suggests the presence of fleas, mites, ringworm, allergies, or a poor diet. Note the type of coat, as well. The proper texture for a Cairn is straight, hard, and dense. It should closely cover the body with only a hint of waviness. Occasionally, a puppy will have a fluffy coat that is quite appealing to buyers. A soft-coated Cairn is nearly impossible to prepare for the show ring. Because the coat lacks its normal weather-resistant properties, even routine grooming is difficult to manage.

If you're uncertain which youngster to choose, don't hesitate to enlist the breeder's help.

Purchasing Your Cairn

After you have selected the Cairn Terrier you want to take home, it's time to discuss the conditions of sale with the breeder. Most breeders provide written contracts that outline the terms. If they grade a puppy as pet quality, for instance, breeders usually require that it be neutered before they release the AKC papers. Some give limited registration, which means the dog is registered with the American Kennel Club, but future litters are ineligible. Although Cairns with limited privileges cannot compete in the show ring, they may participate in a variety of other activities.

CARING FOR YOUR CAIRN TERRIER

Preparing for Arrival

Your Cairn Terrier's natural curiosity, combined with its keen senses of smell, hearing, and sight, will lead it to investigate every corner of its home and backyard. Because dogs cannot distinguish between acceptable playthings and objects that could harm them, you'll need to begin terrier-proofing your environment long before you bring your new pet home. An important decision is where your Cairn will eat, play, and sleep. Dogs generally prefer to remain near family members—their new pack—so many owners select the kitchen for their pets' quarters. The floor is stain resistant and washable, and doorways can be blocked with doggie gates.

To check the area for hidden dangers, get down to your dog's eye (and nose) level. Any tempting aromas coming from the garbage can? Shoes, socks, or clothing left out? Valuables that could be destroyed? Place as much out of reach as possible, but remember that Cairns are expert climbers and jumpers. Left-

This bright-eyed fellow exemplifies one canine historian's description of the breed: "The Cairn Terrier expression is a mixture of jolliness and wickedness, with that 'varminty' note so much desired."

overs on the kitchen table, for instance, quickly will disappear in the presence of these clever little terriers. Don't leave chocolate around the house; it can be harmful and even deadly to dogs. Also, look for any household products that could hurt your Cairn, such as cleaning agents, insecticides, rodent traps, and electric cords. Several varieties of house plants, if ingested, cause illness—even death—in pets. Be careful with medicines, matches, cigarettes, candy, and alcoholic beverages, as well. Keep the toilet bowl covered, especially if you use chemicals or disinfectants. Don't allow your Cairn near open stairways, unscreened windows, or balconies.

Because Cairns will take off at the first sign of potential prey, deaf to your commands to come back, a secure fence or fully enclosed kennel run is essential. In fact, breeders often insist on fenced-in backyards or regular on-leash walks as a condition of sale. Carefully examine your property for chemicals and poisons that could sicken your Cairn. If you treat your lawn with fertilizers or insecticides, wait the allotted time before you let your dog play outside. Certain plants, including hollies, privet hedges, azaleas, English ivy, wild mushrooms, and flower bulbs, can cause life-threatening reactions if dogs swallow parts. Depending on where you live, poisonous toads, snakes, hawks, large owls, and coyotes also might pose risks. Perhaps the best way to ensure your Cairn's safety when it plays outdoors is to never leave it unattended. Stray animals might come into the yard, possibly to fight. Also, the theft of purebred dogs is a problem in some parts of the country.

Preparing your surroundings for the arrival of a Cairn Terrier is, in many ways, like planning for a new baby. Yet, with dedication and diligence, coupled with a sense of humor, you can protect youngsters from dangers they are unable to sense themselves.

Your New Cairn Terrier

When your Cairn Terrier is old enough to leave the litter, usually between 8 and 12 weeks of age, the breeder will contact you to make arrangements for you to pick up your puppy. The best time to introduce it to its new home is over a long weekend or vacation period, so you'll have plenty of time to spend

with it. Of course, avoid hectic family holidays like Thanksgiving and Christmas. These are the worst times to bring home a pet. If you plan to transport your Cairn by car, take along an airline-style carrier for the ride home. For safety's sake, secure the crate to your car's back seat with the seat belt. Place an old blanket and newspapers inside. To make the trip as pleasant as possible, speak quietly and reassuringly to your pet. Let it know it's joining a family who will love and adore it. Play soft music on the car radio. Once home, let it relieve itself (in the place to which you want it to return) before you take it inside. Provide free access to drinking water, but let it calm down awhile before you feed it.

Your Cairn probably will want to explore its territory, but don't allow it to become overtired from vigorous playing. Also, wait a few days before you throw a puppy party for friends and neighbors to welcome the newcomer. Puppies, as well as adult dogs, often feel insecure in strange environments and temporarily may prefer the seclusion of their crates. Some even skip a meal or two, but it's no cause for concern. If your Cairn whines at night, move its crate next to your bed. Not only will your presence soothe the youngster, but also you'll be available to let it out when needed. Don't relent and take your Cairn to bed with you unless you want to share the blankets forever. Remain firm in your resolve and you'll find it will settle

How many hazards can you find in this picture? Turn to page 91 to find the answer.

down by the second or third night. Although adding a new pet to the household is difficult and stressful, at times, for both you and your dog, you'll soon wonder how you ever got along without the friendship of this spunky fellow.

Crate Training

Resembling the hidden dens of their wild canine ancestors, crates offer a sense of security to dogs. Crates protect puppies when they must be left alone, and provide safe havens where dogs can relax undisturbed. Most Cairn Terriers readily adjust to their crates. In fact, many breeders will have already trained their puppies to stay through the night in their crates before they send them to their new homes. By confining puppies to their instinctive nesting areas, crates aid in the task of housebreaking while they minimize chewing and other destructive behaviors. Crates also afford peace of mind to owners when they cannot supervise their dogs.

To successfully introduce your Cairn to its crate, make the task as pleasant as possible. Never scold it during training or confine it as punishment. Also, teach children not to disturb the dog in its crate. Have the crate set up and in place when you bring your pet home. A wire pen is easy to fold down for travel, while an airline-style carrier is easy to clean and sanitize. Be sure the crate is the correct size. Some owners purchase pens that are too large so their dogs will have plenty of room. However, this defeats their purpose for housebreaking because puppies have enough space to relieve themselves and still keep their beds clean. Look for a crate that is approximately 23 inches

Supplies for Your Cairn Terrier
- ◆ Bowls for food and water
- ◆ Food, quality brand
- ◆ Brush, comb, toenail clippers
- ◆ Dog crate
- ◆ Bedding, old blankets or towels
- ◆ Toys
- ◆ Newspapers, paper towels
- ◆ Urine cleaner (odor neutralizer)
- ◆ Collar, leash, name tag
- ◆ Reference books

(57.5 cm) wide by 30 inches (75 cm) long by 24 inches (60 cm) high. (Ask the breeder's advice if you're uncertain what to select.) Place a cushion and soft blanket inside.

To coax your pet to enter, leave the door open and put a favorite toy or treat in the crate. Give a specific command, such as "go to bed," and praise lavishly when it obeys. When your Cairn feels comfortable inside, close the door for a minute or two. Speak softly and reassuringly. If it behaves, open the door and give plenty of praise. If it whines, tell it "No!" and ignore it until it calms down. Gradually lengthen the time your Cairn stays in its crate. You'll soon find it enters without protest whenever it wants quiet time away from the bustle of its active household. Remember, the crate is your Cairn's private sanctuary and all family members should respect it as such.

Safe Toys

Cairn Terriers are playful and happy-go-lucky little dogs, so it's essential to provide an array of safe toys. These include durable rubber balls, rope toys with knots at both ends, and the

This well-supervised Cairn beats the "dog days" of summer by floating in its backyard swimming pool.

and swallow pieces of the toys. This can lead to choking and intestinal blockages, which are veterinary emergencies. If you want to give a special treat, try one of the chewies made of compressed ground rawhide or vegetable products. The small, easy-to-digest particles allow pets to consume them safely.

Be sure to spend time, one-on-one, with your Cairn. Toss a ball and train it to bring it back to you. Show your pet how to find a hidden treat by using its nose to discover the hiding place. Teach it the names of its toys. You'll be amazed to watch as your dog searches the entire house for its "ball" or "bone." Doggie

nearly indestructible Kongs. Cairns are particularly fond of fuzzy balls, fabric throwing discs, and fleece animal-shaped toys. However, be careful of rawhides and bones, as well as soft-rubber squeaky toys. With their large teeth and powerful jaws, Cairns easily can shred, splinter,

To prevent escapes by digging or climbing, a securely fenced yard like this one is essential.

"Anchors aweigh!" This canine sailor awaits the catch of the day in its favorite place on the family boat.

play sessions not only entertain and relieve boredom, but also develop self-confidence and stimulate learning. They serve as valuable first steps in preparing for all forms of Obedience competition, as well.

AKC Registration
When you purchase your Cairn from the breeder, make certain you receive an application, or "blue slip," to register the dog with the American Kennel Club. After you have chosen a name, complete the form and return it to the AKC with the proper fee. If you plan to enter your Cairn in dog shows or Obedience trials, you or the breeder may want the kennel name included as part of your dog's name. If the breeder has a registered kennel name, he or she must sign the form before you may use the name. After the AKC processes the application, you'll receive your Cairn's formal registration certificate. Only AKC registered dogs are eligible to participate in the organization's activities. However, the club also grants Indefinite Listing Privileges to unregistered dogs, such as rescue animals, so they may compete in Obedience and Performance events.

Identification Methods
Few things strike greater fear in the heart of an owner than discovering an open gate and realizing a pet is missing. Because Cairns are noted escape artists, able to squeeze through the tiny crevices, it's important to properly identify your dog as soon as you bring it home. Currently, three methods are available: ID tags, tattoos, and microchips. All dogs need basic tags, even when they have permanent forms of identification. People who find stray animals usually check first for collar tags. Information on the tag can include your name and address, or the telephone number of a national lost pet registry service. Using a third-party listing instead of your own protects your privacy and avoids nuisance calls from those who prey on peoples' misfortunes.

However, because collars can break and ID tags can be lost, many owners prefer to use tattoos or microchips to distinguish their Cairns. In fact, your puppy may already have one of these forms of identification when it comes from the breeder. Both methods are safe, easy to perform, and well tolerated. Veterinarians can tattoo code numbers on a pet's inner thigh or abdomen in less than 15 minutes, usually without anesthesia. They also can insert microchips, which resemble grains of rice, with a syringe.

HOW-TO: TRAVELING

The Cairn Terrier's lively and inquisitive nature, coupled with its portable size, makes it a perfect companion on family vacations. Yet, whether your plans include a weekend getaway or the Grand Tour, you'll need to begin preparations early if you want your dog to accompany you on your journey. First, schedule an appointment with the veterinarian to make certain your Cairn is fit to travel. Be sure all vaccinations are current, as well. Most destinations require a health certificate, signed within 10 days of the departure date. Even if you travel within the United States, a health certificate will allow you to board your dog for the day at the kennel facilities of major tourist sites.

If you plan to travel abroad, find out the destination country's entry requirements for pets. Great Britain, as well as a number of other countries, require a six-month quarantine for all incoming dogs. Hawaii is off-limits to vacationing pets, too, because of its quarantine. Be sure to verify the policies of airlines, ships, trains, or buses well in advance. Finally, pack all necessary supplies, including enough food to last throughout the trip.

Although traveling with a pet is more complicated than touring solo, with adequate preparation you'll find it a rewarding experience—with memories that will last a lifetime. Bon voyage!

On the Road

Most Cairns love to ride in the car and have learned to pick up their owners' subtle signals of an impending excursion. They greet the jingling of keys, for instance, with wagging tails and excited barks that say, "Don't forget me!" To condition your pet to car travel, start at an early age. Begin with short rides and try to avoid unpleasant experiences. Be sure to praise and reward proper behavior. Train your Cairn to ride in a crate, fastened securely with the seat belt. If your car has a passenger-side air bag, have your dog ride in the back seat. The abrupt deployment of an air bag could injure or kill your dog. Never open the car door, especially in unfamiliar places, until your dog is safely leashed. It takes only a moment for a dog to escape! **Never leave your dog in a parked car in warm weather.** Even in the shade, a closed car quickly can reach oven-like temperatures that

may lead to heat stroke and death in pets.

Flying High

Although airlines successfully transport thousands of animals each year, including top show dogs, the potential hazards of shipping by air concern all owners. Fortunately, the Cairn's size enables it to travel in the passenger cabin, as long as it fits into an underseat crate or other airline-approved carrier. Many travelers have invested in soft-sided carriers. These zippered bags also serve as convenient totes on tours or as pets' private sleeping bags. Because only one animal is permitted in each section of the plane, make your reservations as early as possible. Try to book a direct flight and avoid weekend or holiday travel, if possible.

If you must ship your dog as cargo, contact the airline well in advance of your departure to make your reservations and verify regulations. Use only airline-approved crates that meet the standards of the Animal and Plant Health Inspection Service. Choose a crate with enough room for your Cairn to stand, lie down, and turn around, but not so large that it's bumped around within the crate during the flight. All crates need at least a one-inch rim around the outside to prevent luggage from blocking the air vents. On the day of the flight, don't feed within six hours or give water within two hours. Arrive early and let your dog relieve itself before it gets into its crate. Make certain airline personnel know that a dog is on board, and find out whether your pet has been safely loaded before you get on the plane. Copies of the Animal Welfare Act, which regulates air shipments of animals, are available from the U.S. Department of Agriculture.

Cruising With Your Cairn

Currently, the only cruise ship that accepts dogs is Cunard Line's Queen Elizabeth 2. Although pets are not permitted in staterooms, they are cared for in the ship's kennels by trained "kennel maids." Owners may visit their dogs and take them for walks in special runs. The QE2's kennels accommodate only 14 animal passengers, so be sure to reserve your Cairn's place as early as possible. Check with the destination country to confirm that dogs are welcome. A cruise is an ideal way to transport a dog from abroad to the United States, but remember that Great Britain subjects all incoming dogs to lengthy quarantine.

Trains and Buses

In the United States, trains and buses don't allow dogs to accompany their owners or to travel as baggage. Regulations vary in other countries.

Hotel Accommodations

To locate accommodations that welcome pets, consult a knowledgeable travel agent, the American Automobile Association (AAA), or the guidebook, *Touring with Towser*. Don't overlook bed and breakfasts, country inns, or mountain

Health Certificate

Always travel with an up-to-date copy of your Cairn Terrier's health certificate. Information should include the following:
- Your name and address
- Pet's name, species, and breed
- Date of rabies inoculation, type of vaccine, serial number of rabies tag
- Statement that your dog is free of, and has not been exposed to, contagious diseases, and does not come from a rabies-quarantined area or an area where rabies is known to exist
- Veterinarian's signature

cabins. A number of privately owned lodgings cater to well-behaved canine guests. Some advertise in the classified sections of dog magazines. Always verify the establishment's pet policy in advance, even if you have stayed there before. Let management know your dog will be crated when you are away from your room.

Some lucky Cairns travel by ship.

BASIC TRAINING

Known for its intelligence and eagerness to please, the Cairn Terrier readily masters not only the basic commands, but also an array of tricks that charm as well as challenge its owners. Yet, the quickness with which it learns soon leads to boredom, so it's important to keep lessons short and interesting. A Cairn won't tolerate the endless repetition of exercises like some of the more biddable breeds. Its refusal to perform leads some observers to view it as independent and stubborn. A common complaint among owners is that it obeys only when it chooses to do so. Unless you establish and enforce the rules of proper behavior from the beginning, you'll likely find your dog is running the household. However, because it thrives on its owner's attention and approval, a Cairn often loses heart with harsh rebukes or physical discipline. According to Mrs. Byron Rogers, author of the 1922 handbook, *Cairn and Sealyham Terriers*, "There is no dog in the world easier to teach, if rightly handled, for he responds to every tone of the voice and when he recognizes displeasure he never forgets it." If reprimanded, the dog's "whole heart is put into the task of remembering not to bring back the tone that hurt him," she adds. Because of its sensitive nature, a Cairn reacts better to rewards—praise, petting, and occasional treats—when it obeys, rather than

Try rewards, such as praise, petting, and occasional treats, to reinforce proper behavior.

punishment when it misbehaves. Positive reinforcement, combined with consistent training, will allow your Cairn Terrier to develop into a well-mannered member of the household.

House-training

The first task your Cairn must learn is the proper place to relieve itself. Although some owners put down newspapers indoors, it's easier for puppies to master the idea of house-training when they start from the beginning with outdoor training. As soon as you bring your new puppy home, take it to the spot to which you want it to return. Its scent will remain and help to remind it of its "business." Most Cairns—even youngsters—quickly grasp the concept of house-training. However, to ensure your Cairn's success, it's vital to take an active role in the training process.

Monitor Carefully

Watch your puppy closely and be ready to take it out whenever it indicates by sniffing, whining, or circling that it needs to go. Have its leash handy and carry the puppy to the desired place. Choose a special command—one that you're not embarrassed to say in public—and give it each time you want your puppy to eliminate. Praise lavishly when it obeys. It's important to respond to your puppy's signals, even if you think it doesn't need to go. This helps to reinforce your puppy's wish to alert you.

Be Consistent

Always feed and water at the same times each day, and follow a regular schedule of walks. Also, take your puppy outside as soon as it awakens in the morning, after naps and play sessions, and right before bedtime. You might have to take it out during the night as well, until it develops greater control of its bladder. Puppies often need to go out every hour or two, so don't disregard their warnings.

Crate Your Pup

Because dogs instinctively prefer to keep their sleeping quarters clean, crating allows owners to determine when, as well as where, their puppies will eliminate. Set up the crate in the kitchen or family room, where you can watch for signs that it needs to go out. Take your puppy to the same spot each time, and give plenty of praise when it performs. If it doesn't go, take it back to its crate. This helps to prevent the problem of the puppy coming inside and then urinating on the floor.

Accidents

Of course, all puppies have occasional accidents, so don't scold your Cairn unless you catch it in the act. Because it has a short memory, it won't be able to associate your displeasure with its mistake. Never follow the suggestion of rubbing the puppy's nose in its mess. Such cruelty won't achieve any meaningful results. To prevent future accidents, use a commercial enzyme-neutralizing odor and stain remover to clean the spot and remove all traces of odor. Some adult dogs have difficulty with housebreaking, possibly due to physical problems, and may continue to have accidents indoors. However, don't lose hope. Most Cairns are fully housebroken by the time they are two years old.

Basic Commands

You can begin to teach the basic commands—come, sit, down, stay, and heel—when your puppy is about four months old. However, don't expect perfect performance at this point. Most Cairn Terriers don't succeed at competitive obedience until a year or two, when they start to develop greater concentration. To avoid confusing your puppy with multiple demands, practice one exercise at a time. Also, involve only one family member in training. Because terriers are easily distracted, work indoors or in a confined area until your puppy has mastered the command. Keep sessions short—10 to 15 minutes, at most. Ideally, you should end while your puppy is still eager to learn.

When you give a command, speak in a normal tone of voice and don't whisper or shout. Give the direction once, then wait a few seconds for your puppy to obey. Always use the same word each time you train. It's impossible for puppies to grasp complicated phrases. When it performs correctly, praise with a heartfelt, "Good Girl!" or "Good Boy!" Whether or not you reward with food is a personal decision. However, the breed is highly motivated to learn nearly any feat for a doggie treat. If you do use treats, give them only during the learning phase of the exercise. Later, use praise and petting as rewards. End each lesson on a positive note with a task your puppy can do well. Follow with a brief play period or walk around the block. Always keep training sessions fun for your dog. Never lose your temper or resort to physical discipline. When training a puppy—

Come. Show your puppy its favorite toy to coax it to come to you.

especially a terrier—maintain a sense of humor. It won't take long to discover that your little Cairn has one!

Training Equipment

Before you start, you'll need two pieces of equipment: a well-fitting collar and a 6-foot (18 m) leash. Some instructors suggest using a choke collar that tightens briefly during corrections. However, a puppy should always start with a buckle-style collar, which is more comfortable and less restrictive. Choose one made of nylon, rather than leather, so it won't feel stiff or bulky. Avoid fancy rhinestone-studded neckwear during training sessions. If you decide to try a choke collar, look for nylon fabric or a fine link chain. To determine the correct size, measure around your Cairn's neck and add two or three inches. For example, if the total is 12 inches (30 cm), you'll need to purchase a size 12 collar. Order an ID tag as soon as you obtain a collar. Also, look for a leash made of cotton or nylon fabric. Leather and chain leashes are not suitable for training. Retractable leashes work well for casual strolls—and for teaching your puppy to come when called—but you'll need a basic leash for the heel exercise and formal walks. Be sure to allow time for your puppy to adjust to its collar and leash before you begin training. Fasten the collar loosely for a day or two. Then, attach a lightweight leash and let it drag on the ground while your Cairn plays. Keep an eye on your puppy, though, so the leash doesn't become tangled.

Come: All dogs must learn to come when called. No other lesson is more vital to your Cairn's safety. To start this exercise, have your dog sit or stand next to you. Step back a couple of feet and give the command, "Come!" Use your Cairn's name as part of the command. For example, "Sparky, Come!" This attracts its attention, so it will be ready for the signal that follows. Open your arms or gently clap your hands to encourage it to come. You also can teach this exercise by using a retractable leash to carefully reel in your dog. Praise enthusiastically when your Cairn comes to you. However, never call it to you for punishment. Make a game of the *come* command by having family members sit on the floor and take turns calling and petting your dog. Cairns love to be the center of attention! Always start training indoors or in a confined area. When it performs reliably, move outdoors where it will face greater distractions. Because Cairns have a tendency to come only when they want to, you must insist that your puppy obey right from the start. Mischievous antics might be cute, but if you accept them you'll only reinforce negative behavior.

Sit: Most Cairns learn the *sit* command with little difficulty. To begin, kneel beside or in front of your dog. Give the command, "Sit!"

Sit. Carefully push down on the hindquarters while pressing back on the chest.

Stay: With your Cairn in the sit or down position, give the command, "Stay!" Then, take a step or two forward and turn to face your dog. Don't stare into its eyes, though, because animals often take this as a threat. Instead of helping it to remain still, it may cause it to move due to anxiety. Hold the position for only a few seconds. Give a release word such as "Okay!" or "Done!" to finish the exercise. Gradually increase the length of time your Cairn remains in position, as well as the distance you move away. To reinforce the *stay* command, make a game of it. Place your Cairn in a sit-stay, for instance, while you hide a treat in another room. Call your dog to you (now it knows how to come) and show it how to find the treat.

Then, gently push down on its hindquarters with one hand as you press back on its chest with the other. You also can push inward on the backs of its knees to have it sit. Praise it when it obeys, even if it holds the position for only a moment. Train your Cairn to sit straight, rather than lean on one hip with a leg out to the side, if you plan to compete in Obedience.

Down: Start with your Cairn in the sit position, described above. Give the command, "Down!" Then, carefully push down on its upper back with one hand as you extend its front legs with the other. You also can pat the floor or place a treat on the floor to encourage it to lie down. Praise enthusiastically when it performs correctly. Some Cairns don't like this exercise, so work on the command whenever you want your dog to lie quietly by your side.

Heel: Cairns attract a lot of attention when they go out in public, so it's important to teach your dog to walk properly on a leash without pulling or lagging. To start, have your Cairn sit or stand next to your left hip. This is correct heel position. Give the command, "Heel!" Then, step out on your left foot. Keep the leash tight during the initial phase of training, so your dog maintains the correct position. If it forges ahead, tell it "Heel!" and gently snap the leash. If it lags behind, encourage it by calling its name or patting your left leg. Praise generously when your

Down. Starting from the sit position, gently extend the front legs while pushing down on the back.

This Cairn is answering its owner's "Come!"—the most important command your dog will learn.

Cairn walks nicely by your side. You also might try a whistle-like training device, sold in pet supply stores, which attaches between the collar and leash. The beeping sound that it emits whenever your dog pulls on the leash acts as an automatic correction. To improve its skills and keep its attention, alternate your pace between fast and slow speeds. Add some right, left, and about turns, as well. If you plan to compete in formal Obedience, you'll also need to work on off-lead heeling. Always practice in a confined area. Start with the leash dragging

Stay: After your Cairn understands this command, gradually lengthen the time before you give the release word.

on the ground, so you'll have some control. Later, when it obeys reliably, remove the leash. If your Cairn has difficulty with off-lead heeling, go back to an earlier stage of training and proceed at whatever pace it takes to successfully master the exercise. Be patient with your Cairn Terrier, and give plenty of praise when it performs correctly.

Correcting Problem Behavior

A Vocal Breed

An important part of its working ability was the Cairn Terrier's use of vocalizations to alert its master to the position of quarry deep within the rocky crevices of Scotland's cliffs and cairns. The earliest known reference to "voice" was found in Oliver Goldsmith's treatise, published in 1774, which recognized that terriers not only pursued their prey by sight and scent, but also "[gave] notice by their barking in what part of the [burrow] the fox or badger [resided]." Today, though it no longer aids the sportsman in his quest for prey, the Cairn remains an attentive watchdog with an array of vocal tones at its disposal. However, most are not problem barkers, but warn only of unusual sights and sounds. Some even distinguish between regular visitors and strangers, and remain silent at the approach of familiar guests. To develop your Cairn's innate talent as a watchdog, allow it to bark several times to alert you. Then, tell it "Quiet!" or "Enough!" Praise it when it stops barking, even for a moment. Have your dog sit by your side when you answer the doorbell. This often helps dogs to better control their barking. You may need to set up practice "visitor" sessions with a cooperative neighbor to reinforce your Cairn's training.

Destructive Chewing

Cairns may begin the destructive habit of chewing between four and seven months of age, when their gums ache from the teething process. Furniture, carpets, shoes, and socks become favorite targets when puppies are left to their own devices. To relieve the discomfort that accompanies the emergence of adult teeth, be sure to offer stiff rubber-like chew toys, hard biscuits, or other sturdy playthings. One owner suggested giving a chilled Kong toy filled with a dab of peanut butter. Chewing on a frozen wet washcloth also helps to ease a puppy's sore mouth. Perhaps the best way to prevent problem chewing is to keep valuables off the floor and crate your puppy when you're unable to supervise it. If you catch it with an unacceptable object, give a firm "Leave It!" and show it its own toy. Repeat this process until your puppy understands the difference between its possessions and yours. Always reward good behavior with praise and petting. Never punish long after the fact. You may need to use an unpleasant-tasting repellent, such as Bitter Apple, on items that your puppy persistently chews. Most Cairns outgrow this phase, but some go through a second stage of chewing between seven and twelve months.

Born to Dig

Bred for centuries to go to ground in search of prey, Cairns are natural diggers. With their strong legs, large feet, and sturdy toenails, they miss no opportunity to rid their backyards of pesky mice, squirrels, and other small animals. Not to be deterred by treasured plantings or verdant lawns, these little earth dogs pursue their quarry with admirable persistence. They also delight in using potted house plants as choice spots in which to bury favorite toys. To combat the problem, watch your dog closely when it plays outdoors. Boredom is usually a factor in destructive digging, so make certain your Cairn receives adequate daily exercise. Some owners fill the "craters" their pets leave behind with water or small stones. Because digging is an instinctive trait, though, you might consider setting aside a separate area of your yard where your dog safely can dig to its heart's content. For a special treat, plant a little surprise for your dog to find!

Nipping

Puppies use their mouths, as well as their noses, to explore and interpret their surroundings. When they nip at their owners' hands and feet, or grasp at their clothing, they are usually trying to signal that they want to play. (Watch how young littermates interact with one another.) Of course, puppy teeth are sharp and dog bites painful, so this form of communication must be redirected as soon as possible toward more acceptable behaviors. Whenever your puppy nips at you, give a sharp "No!" and present it with one of its toys. Praise generously if it takes the toy. Be patient during this stage of learning. Always have a toy on hand to distract your puppy's attention, but avoid games like tug-of-war that may encourage nipping and biting.

The AKC's Canine Good Citizen Program

This certificate program, created in 1989 by the American Kennel Club, encourages responsible pet ownership and mastery of the basic commands. Points the evaluator considers include: Would the dog be a reliable family member? Does it exhibit good manners in public? Has it been conditioned to the presence of other dogs? To qualify for the CGC Certificate, your Cairn Terrier must pass each of the 10 parts of the test, which the judge scores on a pass or fail basis. The test is not a competition, and does not require the precise execution of formal obedience exercises.

The Canine Good Citizen Test

1. **Accepting a Friendly Stranger:** Demonstrates that your dog will allow a friendly stranger to approach it and speak to you in a natural, everyday situation.
2. **Sitting Politely for Petting:** Demonstrates that your dog will allow a friendly stranger to touch it when the two of you are out together.
3. **Appearance and Grooming:** Demonstrates that your dog will welcome being groomed and examined, and will permit a stranger, such as a veterinarian, groomer, or friend of yours, to do so.
4. **Out for a Walk:** Demonstrates that you have physical control of your dog.
5. **Walking Through a Crowd:** Demonstrates that your dog can move about politely in pedestrian traffic and is under control in public places.
6. **Sit and Down on Command/Staying in Place:** Demonstrates that your dog has been trained, will respond to your command to sit and down, and will remain in the place you command it.
7. **Coming When Called:** Demonstrates that your dog will come when called.
8. **Reaction to Another Dog:** Demonstrates that your dog can behave politely around other dogs.
9. **Reactions to Distractions:** Demonstrates that your dog is confident at all times when faced with common distracting situations, such as the dropping of a large book or a jogger running in front of it.
10. **Supervised Separation:** Demonstrates that your dog can be left alone, if necessary, and will maintain its training and good manners.

GROOMING AND COAT CARE

The Layered Look

Working on the misty banks and braes of Scotland more than two hundred years ago, the Cairn Terrier was known for its close-fitting, weather-resistant coat. "Many a weary long walk they had in snow and sleet," wrote canine historian Walter Hutchinson, "so that a warm jacket and stout hide were necessary." The profuse, harsh outer layer protected the dog from the drenching rains that swept in from the Atlantic Ocean, while the short, soft, close, furry undercoat offered insulation against the region's frigid temperatures. The coat shielded the dog from thorns, sharp rocks, and the nips of its quarry, as well.

Today, though the Cairn no longer trudges through peat bogs or into sea-swept crevices in pursuit of otters, badgers, and foxes, it continues to maintain its distinctive, double-coated mantle. To keep the coat in peak condition, begin routine grooming as soon as your puppy joins the household. This should include regular brushing, toenail clipping, teeth cleaning, skin and ear care when required, and occasional baths. Hand stripping, or plucking, also must be done periodically to remove dead hair and permit the emergence of a healthy new coat.

Note the desirable dark points on the muzzle and ears.

Grooming Basics

The earlier you begin simple grooming tasks, the easier it will be to train your pet to accept all forms of handling. In fact, most members of the canine family consider grooming a natural, instinctive behavior. If you have more than one dog, for instance, you'll often see them licking and cleaning each other. Although grooming may seem time consuming and complicated, it not only improves the dog's appearance, but also plays a major role in good health. The attention you give your Cairn will allow you to notice changes quickly and obtain prompt veterinary care when needed.

Brushing

The most important part of grooming is consistent brushing. A Cairn requires fewer baths when its hair is brushed at least several times a week. Regular brushing distributes the natural oils throughout the coat that give it the ability to shake off water. It keeps the skin healthy by stimulating blood circulation and encourages new hair growth. Brushing also minimizes the problems associated with seasonal shedding of the undercoat.

To properly care for the coat, you'll need a pin brush or natural-bristle brush, and a fine-toothed comb. Avoid slicker brushes, though, because they pull out too much "live" hair.

Grooming Equipment

- Pin brush or bristle brush
- Fine-toothed metal comb
- Shampoo formulated for harsh coats
- Waterless shampoo
- Nail clipper or electric nail groomer
- Metal nail file
- Toothbrush and toothpaste
- Ear cleaning solution
- Cotton balls
- Stripping knife
- Thinning shears
- Blunt-tipped scissors

To begin brushing, stand your dog on a grooming table or other convenient surface. Take a small section of hair, parting it if necessary, and brush all the way to the skin. Brush with the hair growth to remove tangles, then go against the growth. This will help to loosen dead hair and dandruff. Finish by brushing once again with the growth pattern. After you have carefully gone over the coat, comb through it to check for tangles. This also helps to remove the fluffy undercoat that is shed in the spring and fall.

Develop a routine that you use each time you brush your Cairn. For example, start with the back and rear legs and finish with the head and chest. Inspect the skin for signs of allergies or parasites, and examine the eyes and ears for discharge or odor. Always keep grooming sessions short and pleasant, for your dog as well as yourself. Finish with praise and a treat. Remember, your little Cairn wants to please you. With gentleness, patience, and persistence, you'll have a pet that not only tolerates but also enjoys being groomed.

Bath Time

Think of your Cairn's coat as a specially designed storm jacket and you'll understand why excessive bathing is harmful. The detergents in shampoos cause the outer coat to lose its natural oils, along with its ability to protect against rain, sleet, and snow. Frequent use of shampoos also loosens the coat, leading to a blousy effect, and dries out the hair and skin. Many Cairns develop skin problems, allergies, and doggie odor when they are bathed too often.

Of course, because Cairns love to romp and play outdoors, there are times when washing is a necessity. Be sure to assemble your supplies—shampoo, washcloth, towels, faucet attachment, nonslip mat, and hair dryer—so you won't have to look for them with a wet dog in tow. A shampoo formulated for terriers or harsh-coated dogs helps to maintain the proper coarse texture of the coat. Most Cairns readily take to the water. They enjoy swimming or splashing in kiddie pools—even joining children in their bathtubs! However, if your pet seems

Brush daily with a pin brush or natural-bristle brush.

Lather thoroughly, but avoid getting soapy water in your dog's eyes or ears. Rinse until the water runs clear and the hair feels "squeaky clean."

apprehensive, speak softly and reassuringly to make the experience as agreeable as possible.

To begin the bath, stand your dog on a non-slip mat in the sink or tub. Thoroughly wet the coat with tepid, never hot, water. Apply a dab of shampoo to the dog's back and develop a good lather. Make certain to soap right down to the skin. Working from back to front, wash the rear legs, feet, and tail. Then, move to the chest, belly, and front legs. After you complete the body, carefully wet the head. Don't let water get in the eyes, ears, or nostrils. Some owners place cotton balls in their dogs' ears to protect the canals from soapy water. Clean the face with a wet washcloth. The most important stage of the bath is the rinse. Allow the water to run clear, washing away all soapy residue. Finally, wrap a large towel around your dog and pat it dry. To guard against chilling, you'll need to use a hair dryer set on low. Hold the dryer with one hand as you brush with the other. Move the dryer over the coat until your dog is completely dry. Dry with the direction of hair growth, so your Cairn won't look too fluffy.

Between full baths, which should be given only a few times a year, you can keep your dog fresh and sweet-smelling with modified baths. First, apply a small amount of shampoo to a wet washcloth. Rub the cloth over the entire body, paying special attention to the feet, legs, and belly area. Follow with a clean wet cloth to remove all traces of shampoo. Finally, pat dry with a towel. The booklet, *Cairn Terrier Groom-ing Start to Finish*, published by the Cairn Terrier Club of America, suggests that owners clean the outer coat by lightly spraying it with a mixture of rubbing alcohol and water, or vinegar and water, and brushing with the hair growth. This is an excellent way to prepare dogs for the show ring because it doesn't soften the coat or increase shedding. It can dry the coat, though, so it shouldn't be used for routine grooming. Commercial waterless shampoos and grooming powders also are available in pet supply stores.

Toenail Clipping

Although most Cairns vigorously protest having their toenails clipped, this is a vital aspect of proper maintenance. Ideally, the nail tip should not touch the floor when a dog is standing in a natural pose. Dogs with nails that are too long must walk on their wrists, rather than the pads of their feet, which leads to a distorted gait. Long nails also are more likely to snag or break during play or exercise.

Before you begin, it's important to understand that dogs have a *quick*, or sensitive area containing nerves and blood supply, that runs the length of their nails. It's easy to see the quick through light-colored nails. If your dog has dark nails, however, you may be able to

locate the quick by shining a light through the nail from back to front. The nail will hurt and bleed if you cut to the quick, so clip only the part that curves downward.

To trim your Cairn's toenails, gently but firmly grasp one of its feet. Push away stray hairs, then position the clipper just over the tip of the nail. Close with a firm snap to cut the nail. Never trim more than an eighth of an inch (.25 cm) at a time. If you accidentally nick the quick, apply a pinch of styptic powder to the nail tip until the bleeding stops. After you have clipped all the nails—and the dewclaws, if present—smooth the rough edges with an emery board. Be sure to trim the hair that grows over the footpads to prevent your Cairn from slipping on smooth floors.

This lovely dog displays the natural, rather than highly stylized, appearance inherent to the breed.

Fleas and Ticks

During routine grooming, carefully examine your Cairn's skin. It should be healthy and clean, with no indication of irritation, flaking, or sores. If your dog is scratching more than usual—especially on the rump above the tail—it might have flea bites. However, you probably won't find parasites on your dog. Because fleas are remarkable jumpers, they spend most of their time off the dog, nestled in bedding material, carpets, and grass. Their calling card is black specks of fecal matter they leave behind in the fur. Fleas not only produce acute itching, but also can transmit tapeworms and a variety of diseases. Although most infestations occur in warm, humid climates, fleas also exist in the arid regions of the southwestern United States.

Preventing and eliminating fleas may seem like a never-ending challenge to many pet owners. To win the battle, you must treat both your dog and its surroundings. Effective insecticides include shampoos, dips, powders, foams, and collars. Some products are applied directly to the skin, usually in a spot between the dog's shoulder blades. These reportedly kill fleas within 24 hours, and continue to work for up to three months. The newest advance in controlling fleas is a prescription medicine in the form of a once-a-month tablet given orally to dogs. It works when a female flea bites a treated dog and then passes the active ingredient into her eggs. By curbing a critical step in the reproductive process, flea eggs cannot develop and the life cycle is broken.

Other parasites that feed on dogs include the American dog tick, brown dog tick, and black-legged or deer tick. Ticks can carry Rocky Mountain spotted fever, Lyme disease, and babesiosis, serious diseases that afflict owners as well as their dogs. Their bites also may cause skin irritation, sores, and occasionally tick paralysis. Dogs that spend much of their time outdoors pick up ticks in woods, tall grass, and shrubbery. However, birds, rodents, deer, and other small animals can bring them right into your backyard. Be sure to inspect your Cairn's coat and skin after a walk in woods or fields. If you find a tick, grasp it with tweezers as close to the skin as possible, and pull straight up with steady pressure. Then clean the area with rubbing alcohol. Ask the veterinarian about the best time for a Lyme disease vaccination.

Dental Care

Until recently, many owners were unaware that they needed to brush their pets' teeth. Tartar accumulation leads to gum disease and tooth loss. Also, bacteria that form in the mouth can spread to other parts of the dog's body. This contributes to heart and kidney disease, as well as other serious illnesses. Elderly pets in particular are susceptible to bacteria-related problems. To keep the teeth in good condition, begin regular brushing as soon as the permanent set comes in. Apply a dab of doggie toothpaste to a toothbrush or piece of gauze, and rub it gently over the teeth and gumline. For puppies, use a cat toothbrush that has bristles only at the tip. There are also several rinses on the market.

However, despite the regular care you give at home, some animals have such a problem with tartar deposits that the veterinarian must remove them with special instruments and polishing agents. Because dogs won't hold still to have their teeth cleaned, dental scaling is performed under short-acting anesthesia. Be sure to follow the professional cleaning with consistent brushing at home.

Ear Care

Another area that needs attention is the ears. Are they pink, healthy, and free of odor? Is there any waxy matter or discharge? If your Cairn is scratching its ears or shaking its head, it may have an infection or allergy. Infections often come from water in the ear canals, excess wax, or insect bites. Allergies come from substances in the environment, such as grasses, pollen, or dust mites, or even from the food your dog eats. To keep the ears free of waxy deposits, wipe the outer part of the canal with a cotton ball soaked in ear-cleaning solution.

HOW-TO: STRIP AND TRIM

Hand Stripping

If you examine the outer coat, you'll notice that each hair varies in tone from root to tip, which gives the Cairn a brindled, or shaded, appearance. Clipping or cutting destroys the distinctive color, as well as the texture of the coat. When the dead hair is trimmed, but not removed, the coat becomes soft and loses its water-repellent characteristics. Dogs quickly become dirty when the undercoat is exposed, and some produce excessive dandruff. The best way to keep your Cairn in proper condition—whether you have a pet or show dog—is to hand strip the outer coat every six to eight months. Stripping removes the dead hair, which is ready to come out, and allows the emergence of new, even growth. Dogs that have been stripped also shed less and remain cleaner than clipped dogs, making them suitable for allergy-prone individuals.

Because it may take several days to completely strip a Cairn, most groomers avoid the procedure or charge impressive fees to compensate for the time involved. A few breeders strip their clients' dogs, but most are willing to demonstrate the technique to owners who want to care for their pets at home. Actually, hand stripping is fairly simple when the coat is fully grown and ready to come out. To begin, grasp a few strands between your fingers and pull steadily with the direction of growth. Gently stretch the skin as you release the hairs. Some owners get a better grip on the hair shafts by applying grooming chalk to the coat or dipping their fingers into the chalk first. Others wear rubber fingertip protectors, similar to the ones used by office workers. A stripping knife also helps to remove the outer coat, but be careful not to cut or break the hairs instead of pulling them. Finally, tidy the feet and backs of the ears with thinning shears.

Pet Grooming

Depending on your Cairn's age at the time of purchase, some grooming may already have been completed. Breeders usually neaten the appearance of the ears by removing stray hairs when puppies are about six weeks old. Many also remove the dark, or black, overlay of hairs that starts to loosen at 8 to 12 weeks. This not only gives an attractive look, but also allows the new adult coat to come in properly. The first major grooming, though, takes place when your puppy reaches 8 to 10 months. When the coat starts to "open" and part down the back, it must be completely removed. You may choose to have a professional handle this twice-yearly grooming, but make certain he or she is experienced in hand stripping terrier coats. If you decide to tackle the job yourself, complete the plucking within a few days so the new coat will be an even length. The CTCA suggests that pet owners hand strip the back, neck, and sides, and use thinning shears on the legs and

When the coat begins to look "blousy" and parts down the back, the long, dead strands must be removed by a process called plucking or stripping.

belly. This gives the correct harsh texture to the dog's back, with softer hair everywhere else. The club's grooming guidebook is highly recommended for all Cairn owners (see Information, page 91).

Rolling the Coat

Because show dogs must look their best for competitions that take place throughout the year—and cannot wait several months to grow a perfect coat—most professional handlers and owner/handlers use a process called "rolling the coat" to keep their terriers in top form. This involves plucking all of the long, dead hairs on an ongoing basis at least once or twice a week. Removing only a few hairs at a time and controlling the emergence of new coat ensures that show dogs are always presentable. Handlers also comb out the dead undercoat when it's ready to be shed. However, some Cairns don't have enough thickness or coarseness to permit rolling the coat. Betty E. Marcum, chairman of the CTCA's grooming booklet committee, advises that exhibitors time the full-coat stripping to coincide with the dog's show schedule.

Grooming for the Show Ring

The technical skills and artistic aptitude necessary to present the Cairn Terrier in the show ring take many years, if not a lifetime, to master. Correct grooming not only enhances a dog's strengths, but also helps to disguise its faults. Poor or excessive grooming can destroy the prospects of even a superior specimen. Because its casual appearance is an integral part of breed type, exhibitors must never show their Cairns in the highly stylized fashion of West Highland White Terriers or Scottish Terriers. Early fanciers, in fact, believed the dogs should be exhibited as nature made them—with no artificial grooming other than a good

brushing. "The idea that a working dog must be trimmed, plucked, powdered, and so on, is abhorrent to the minds of most sport-loving people and should be universally condemned," wrote Mrs. Byron Rogers in the first book on the breed. "The test of the worker is to take him out of the earth, brush him, tidy him up, and put him into the ring," she added. "If he can win then, he deserves to do it; for the dog himself is there to be judged as he is."

Although instruction in the finer points of show grooming is beyond the scope of this book, it's important for beginners to be able to visualize the relevant points of the standard, as well as the "perfect" Cairn, during grooming sessions. The breeder is usually the best source of information on proper technique. Also, consider attending CTCA Specialty Shows where you can view dogs from a variety of kennels. Briefly, show preparation involves a combination of rolling the coat and judicious trimming with thinning shears to blend different parts of the coat into each other. The Cairn must have no visible demarcation lines from one part of its body to another, but must possess a well-furnished cloak of medium-length hair.

Never use scissors or thinning shears to groom the head. The dead coat must be pulled by hand.

THE WELL-FED CAIRN

A Food for Every Cairn

To keep your Cairn Terrier healthy and vigorous, it's important to select and feed a high-quality diet. The food must not only provide adequate nutrients for the various functions that take place within the body, but also be formulated for your pet's stage of development. In the past, dogs often consumed a diet based on table scraps and leftovers. Whether or not this offered sufficient nourishment was a hit-or-miss proposition, at best. Within the past several decades, though, breeders and veterinarians have joined forces to help define the nutritional requirements of dogs, and to create appropriate pet foods to meet those needs. Today, with more than 3,000 manufacturers producing 15,000-plus brands of pet food, selecting the correct formula challenges even experienced owners.

How, then, can you choose the best food for your Cairn? Puppies, as well as adults, need six kinds of nutrients: protein, carbohydrates, fat, vitamins, minerals, and water. The term *nutrient* refers to any component that aids in the body's metabolic processes, such as regulating temperature, acting as structural components, or transporting substances throughout the bloodstream. However, depending on your dog's age, activity level, environment, and health status, the amount and balance of these nutrients will differ.

Cairns are healthy dogs with hearty appetites.

The Basic Nutrient Groups

Protein: Found in foods such as beef, chicken, eggs, grains, and soybeans, protein is essential for normal growth, muscle and bone formation, tissue repair, and internal body functions. Protein constitutes the basic structure of skin, hair, and toenails. It also makes up tendons, ligaments, and muscles. During digestion, protein is broken down into smaller substances called amino acids. The body produces some of these, while the diet supplies others. Most commercial foods use a variety of protein sources to ensure that they provide all the required amino acids. Puppies, active dogs, and nursing mothers need diets that contain between 25 and 30 percent protein. Deficiencies, particularly during growth, may cause skeletal disorders, weight loss, skin and hair problems, and reduced resistance to disease. Excesses, too, may be harmful, especially for senior dogs with reduced kidney function.

Carbohydrates: The carbohydrates from grain and vegetable sources provide your Cairn with energy. The sugar in carbohydrates is carried to the liver, where it's changed into glycogen and stored for later energy demands. Glucose plays a critical role in nourishing the brain because it's one of the few substances that can cross the blood-brain barrier. Dogs develop hypoglycemia when their blood sugar levels become too low, and if the condition is not treated promptly they can go into shock and die. Carbohydrates also supply fiber, which plays a key role in the digestive process. Some forms are useful when dogs have diarrhea or constipation. Others help to lower the level of cholesterol in the blood. Because fiber decreases the absorption of nutrients, puppies and active dogs should avoid diets high in roughage. However, if your dog is overweight, you should feed it a diet with a higher proportion of fiber, which helps it to feel full while it shortens the time food remains in the intestinal tract.

Dietary fat: Fat is a concentrated source of energy that is important during growth, high activity, pregnancy, or when nursing puppies. Fat also aids in the absorption of the fat-soluble vitamins, A, D, E, and K, and supplies the essential fatty acids, linoleic and linolenic acids. Dogs can develop fatty acid deficiencies (FAD) when they consume poor-quality dry foods or diets too low in fat. Signs of FAD include slow growth, reproductive difficulties, weight loss, flaky skin, and dull coat. (You can combat this problem by adding a teaspoon of vegetable oil to your dog's dinner, or by using one of the fatty acid supplements on the market.) Too much fat also is harmful. The most common problem is weight gain. Other conditions that result from an excessive fat intake include pancreatitis (inflammation of the pancreas) and steatorrhea (fat the dog cannot digest, passed in the stool). Because dogs that consume a high-fat diet usually eat less food, nutritional imbalances may occur.

Vitamins: Your dog needs organic compounds for healthy growth and development. Although they don't supply energy directly, vitamins serve as coenzymes that help to regulate various processes within the body. Vitamins are classified into two groups—fat soluble or water soluble—according to the way they are absorbed, stored, and excreted.

Minerals: Less than 1 percent of your dog's weight, they serve a variety of necessary functions: They help to adjust the blood's acid-base balance, maintain the balance of water within the cells, and form the structural components of bones and teeth. Most pet foods supply adequate levels of minerals, so supplementation is usually unnecessary. The most important factor is the *balance* of minerals, especially calcium and phosphorus. Imbalances may lead to lameness, fractures, and abnormal bone development. When you choose a high-quality food, created for your dog's stage of life and activity level, you're providing a diet with the proper level and proportion of minerals.

Water: Your Cairn needs water more than any other nutrient. Although dogs can survive several days without food, a loss of only 10 to 15 percent of body water can lead to illness and even death. Dogs obtain water from drinking, as well as from the water content of their food and the metabolic processes that take place within the body. Because your pet's thirst response will increase or decrease depending on its diet, salt intake, exercise, weather, and temperament, be sure to provide plenty of fresh drinking water. Refill the bowl at least once a day. Your Cairn needs about two-and-a-half times as much water as the amount of dry matter in its dinner. Dogs usually regulate their water intake based on the outflow of fluids from urination, panting, nursing puppies, or vomiting. However, if your Cairn begins to drink more or less than usual, consult the veterinarian.

Types of Dog Food

Dry food: Introduced in the late nineteenth

century as an offshoot of the cereal industry, it is the most popular method of feeding. Most breeders use dry food, and you'll find a number of premium brands in this form. Advantages include convenience, ease of preparation and storage, cost, and easy clean-up, because dogs fed dry food have smaller, firmer stools than dogs that eat moist dog food or table scraps. Because of its low water content, you pay only for the food ingredients themselves, rather than fancy packaging. Most of the nutrients in dry food come from cereal grains, soybeans, vegetables, and meat or chicken meal. Manu-facturers add extra fat, vitamins, and minerals to create a complete balanced diet. Dry food is especially good for the teeth because chewing helps to scrape off plaque and tartar. However, if you're feeding a young puppy, you may want to soften its food first by mixing it with warm water. Problems occur mainly in inexpensive brands, which may be difficult to digest or too low in fat. Always check the expiration date on the package and make certain the bag is in good condition. If fat has soaked through, the food may be contaminated or rancid.

Canned food: Canned food contains mostly meat and meat by-products, along with soy nuggets known as textured vegetable protein. Meat dinners have more protein and fat than other foods, so they are good when your dog's energy needs are high. Although you should avoid feeding canned food exclusively because it may not contain all the required elements, you may add a small amount to dry food to improve its taste. Ration dinners, on the other hand, offer a balanced blend of ingredients, including vitamins and minerals. Depending on the variety you choose, ration products are suitable for all stages of life. Always store

opened cans of food in the refrigerator, and don't leave uneaten food in your dog's bowl.

Soft-moist food: This is a relatively recent addition to the array of pet foods. Shaped like hamburger patties or meat chunks, soft-moist products combine fresh meat with grains or soybeans, vitamins and minerals, fat, and water to form a flavorful, easy-to-digest diet. These foods are convenient to use, simple to store, and travel well. They are ideal for Cairns because most dogs need only one package per feeding. Soft-moist foods also don't require refrigeration. However, manufacturers usually add preservatives and humectants to prevent the products from spoiling and drying. Dogs with sensitivities or allergies may not tolerate these additives, some of which include sugar, and may develop diarrhea or vomiting.

Homemade preparations: With the variety of commercial foods available, there is little reason to cook and prepare food from scratch. Not only is it expensive and time consuming, but also you run the risk of leaving out impor-tant nutrients, overfeeding, or creating foods with serious imbalances. If you insist on fixing your own pet food, be sure to obtain one of the scientific books available and follow the recipes exactly. The textbook *Small Animal Clinical Nutrition III* contains homemade recipes for dogs that require special feeding. (See Information, page 91.) The veterinarian also may have recipes that provide complete and balanced nutrition.

Special diets: Because the food your dog eats plays a critical role in the management and treatment of certain diseases, researchers and manufacturers have developed an assort-ment of special diets, available by prescription from the veterinarian. For example, dogs with kidney disease maintain or improve their condition on meals with lower levels of protein. Dogs with heart failure require reduced-sodium foods. Because these scientifically formulated diets come in convenient dry or canned recipes, you can take a significant step in improving your dog's health with a minimum of effort.

Feeding Your Cairn Terrier

You'll need to regulate the amount of food your dog eats, depending on its activity level, age, and stage of life. Generally, Cairns need 30 to 35 calories per pound of body weight, or about one half to two thirds of a cup of high-quality dry food each day. If your dog is active, involved in a rigorous schedule of competitions, pregnant, or nursing puppies, it needs more food than average. Dogs that are inactive or over-weight require less. Use the feeding recommendations on the package only as a guideline. Your Cairn's physical condition is the ultimate test in deciding how much to feed. Ideally, you should be

able to feel a thin layer of flesh (not fat) covering the ribs, and the hip bones should not be sharp or prominent to your touch. By weighing your dog periodically, you can note any changes and adjust your feeding program accordingly.

Special Nutritional Needs

Puppies

When you purchase your new puppy, one of the supplies you should receive from the breeder is a small amount of the food it has been eating, along with instructions on when and how much to feed. Your Cairn will grow rapidly in its first year, from a bouncing pup to a dignified adult. To make certain it receives the nutrients it needs, choose a food made especially for puppies. It should be energy dense, easy to digest, and at least 29 percent protein. Be sure the label guarantees the food is complete and balanced. Your puppy will need a smaller amount of food if you feed a high-quality brand.

Adult Dogs

When your Cairn approaches its first birthday, you may notice it has begun to reduce its activity level, along with its food intake. This is the time to change your dog's diet to a maintenance formula (see chart, page 50). Whenever you make a feeding change, introduce the new food gradually to avoid causing digestive upsets. Start by mixing one quarter of the adult food with three quarters of the puppy food. Continue

A dog's nutritional status is often reflected in the health of its skin and coat. This Cairn's thick and lustrous fur is a result of eating a well-balanced diet.

to add more of the new dinner until your dog is eating it exclusively. Be sure to have a bowl of water available.

Active Dogs

Few Cairns work for their livings as did their ancestors. However, your dog may expend nearly as much energy when it competes on the show circuit, trains for and performs in Obedience trials, or simply plays in the back-yard. Canned and dry performance foods, with their higher levels of nutrients and easy-to-digest formulas, work well for dogs under both emotional and physical stress. Another way to increase the energy content of the diet is to add one-half to one tablespoon of vegetable oil to your dog's regular dry dinner.

The most important nutrient your dog needs when it's active is water. Dogs don't perspire, but they lose fluid when they pant. Always provide water during and after exercise, competition, or travel.

Overweight Dogs

Although Cairns are active and alert little dogs, they have a tendency to gain weight. In fact, a study done in the United Kingdom a decade ago indicated that Cairn Terriers were the second most likely breed to become obese, after Labrador Retrievers. This may be due to hereditary

Soft, chewy, or crunchy, there's a food formulated for your Carin's nutritional needs.

Feeding Suggestions

◆ Choose a quiet, out-of-the-way place to feed your dog, and always feed it in the same place. Crate feeding may work well.
◆ Don't disturb your dog when it's eating.
◆ Don't serve food directly from the refrigerator or stove. Be careful of foods from the microwave; these may be too hot for your pet.
◆ Give your dog 15 to 20 minutes to eat, then remove any leftover dinner.
◆ If your dog leaves food, feed less next time. If your dog eats all its food and still looks hungry, add more at the next meal.
◆ Always provide fresh drinking water, but don't give your dog cold water; cool is best.
◆ Clean all bowls daily with hot water and soap.

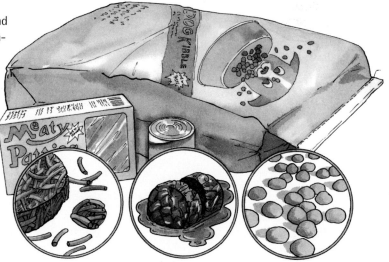

Estimated Energy Content of Dog Foods

Dry food	350 Kcal per 8-ounce cup
Soft-moist	425 Kcal per 6-ounce package
Canned	250 Kcal per 6-ounce can

factors or their hearty appetites. Other causes may include lack of exercise, boredom, and age. Excess weight contributes to heart, liver, and kidney disease; cancer, skin problems, arthritis, and reproductive difficulties. Overweight dogs face greater risks during surgery, both from the procedure itself and the anesthesia. Obesity affects not only the quality of your dog's life, but also its lifespan. If your Cairn needs to lose weight, have the veterinarian perform a thorough checkup. Certain illnesses can cause weight gain, while fluid retention, parasites, and pregnancy are sometimes mistaken for excess weight.

The best way to help your dog lose weight is to combine exercise and a high-fiber, reduced-calorie food designed for overweight dogs. Unless the veterinarian has uncovered a condi-

tion that activity could worsen, take your Cairn for one or two 15- to 20-minute walks each day. Exercise helps to burn calories directly and continues to raise your dog's metabolism during rest. It also improves heart function and prevents the loss of muscle that often accompanies dieting. A daily walk provides a time you and your dog can be together, away from the distractions of a busy household, sharing the pleasure of one another's company.

Senior Dogs

When your Cairn reaches eight or nine years of age, consider switching its diet to a formula for senior dogs. Many complex processes take place during aging, including digestive changes, skin and coat problems, bone and joint disor-

Feedings per Day

Age	Number of Meals per Day
Weaning to 3 months	4
3 to 6 months	3
6 to 12 months	2
Adult maintenance	1 or 2
Sedentary, overweight, and senior	2 (smaller meals)

Factors Affecting Maintenance Energy Requirement

Activity	MER Factor
Growth	
Birth to 3 months	2 times MER
3 to 6 months	1.6 times MER
6 to 12 months	1.2 times MER
Work (1 hour exercise)	1.1 times MER
Gestation	
first 6 weeks	1 times MER
last 3 weeks	1.1 to 1.3 times MER
Peak Lactation	
3 to 6 weeks	2 times MER (4-puppy litter)
	4 times MER (8-puppy litter)
Inactivity	0.8 times MER

ders, and reduced organ function. Older dogs are frequently less active than they once were and begin to put on weight. A few eat less because of dental problems, or changes in their senses of taste and smell. (Feeding canned food or adding warm water to dry food can help this.) Although some older dogs may need reduced levels of protein, phosphorus, sodium, and vitamin D, others require more protein, as well as vitamin A, thiamine, choline, folic acid, niacin, vitamin B_{12}, and vitamin E. Skin and coat problems often improve with fatty acid and zinc supplementation, while arthritis may be helped by adding vitamin C to the diet.

THE FUNDAMENTALS OF HEALTH CARE

Locating a Veterinarian

Whether you're a first-time puppy owner or a veteran of the dog fancy, you'll probably have many questions about the well-being of the little Cairn Terrier entrusted to your care. Because the veterinarian is an important partner in keeping your dog healthy, be sure to choose one before you bring your new pet home. The breeder may suggest a veterinarian, if you're buying locally. Other recommendations may come from dog-owning friends or neighbors, groomers, boarding kennels, or veterinary associations. Also, check the yellow pages for animal clinics near your home.

After you've narrowed your choices to two or three, make an appointment to talk with the doctors and, if possible, tour the areas of the buildings that are open to the public. Observe the hospital environment as well as the staff members. Is this the kind of place you would want to bring your Cairn? Is the building clean,

Don't allow your Cairn to exercise in areas that have been treated with insecticides, herbicides, or various lawn chemicals until at least several rainstorms have made the products harmless. Such compounds have been known to cause seizures, which sometimes last throughout the dog's lifetime.

bright, and relatively free of unpleasant odors? Are the receptionist's duties handled efficiently? Do all employees seem to genuinely care about pets? Are the location and hours convenient? Take your time and don't be afraid to ask questions. Your pet's health depends on the care it receives now and throughout its lifetime.

The First Examination

When you purchase your Cairn from a reputable breeder, you're choosing a puppy with the belief that it's healthy and free of apparent defects. Many breeders provide a guarantee that offers a refund or replacement if a problem is found. It's necessary, therefore, to have your Cairn examined as soon as possible—within 48 to 72 hours. During this visit, the veterinarian will listen to the heart and lungs, inspect the coat and skin, feel for any swellings, go over the legs and joints, and check the eyes, ears, and teeth. Be sure to take any records of prior vaccinations, and bring a fresh stool sample so the technician can test for worms or their eggs. Ask any questions you might have about your Cairn. You'll find it helpful, especially as your pet ages, to keep a record of all exams, noting symptoms, prescribed medications, shots, surgeries, and other procedures. A reference book, such as Dr. Uwe Streitferdt's *Healthy Dog, Happy Dog:*

A Complete Guide to Dog Diseases and Their Treatment, is a must for all owners.

Preventive Care

Vaccinations: Puppies receive temporary immunity to certain infectious diseases at birth from antibodies, or special protein molecules, in their mothers' milk. However, this protection lasts only a few weeks. By the time puppies are about six weeks old, they must develop their own immune systems. Dogs, like humans, form disease-fighting antibodies after exposure to mild or altered forms of antigens. The antibodies then travel throughout the bloodstream, ready to mount an attack if bacteria or viral organisms invade the body. Although a small degree of risk is present in any veterinary procedure, the safest way to expose dogs to these antigens is by a series of controlled vaccinations.

Your puppy will need inoculations every two or three weeks until about 16 to 20 weeks of age. Depending on the diseases that are present where you live, the vaccines may include antigens for distemper, parvovirus, parainfluenza, hepatitis, adenovirus, and rabies. Remember, until it is fully vaccinated, your Cairn is at risk of contracting an infectious illness. Avoid taking your puppy to parks, dog shows, or other places where strange animals gather. After your Cairn reaches adulthood, it's important to schedule yearly booster shots to keep its immune system strong.

Heartworms are responsible for serious illness—even death—in dogs. Transmitted by a mosquito bite, rather than from dog-to-dog contact, the parasites are found throughout the United States and Canada. Heartworms live in the heart and large blood vessels, where they can grow 4 to 12 inches long. This causes damage to the heart, lungs, and blood vessels. Because adult worms often live for several years within a dog's body, they produce thousands of microscopic worms. When a mosquito bites a dog that has these circulating microfilaria, it becomes infected and can transmit the worms to another dog. Both adult and immature heartworms often exist in a dog for years without signs of disease. By the time owners notice coughing, difficulty breathing, or other problems, their pets are seriously ill. Treatment, which is aimed at killing adult as well as microscopic worms, has many potential complications.

Fortunately, heartworms can be prevented with medication. However, dogs that have never taken medication should be tested before they begin the first dose. One kind of test, in which a blood sample is examined under a microscope, shows microfilaria circulating in the bloodstream. This suggests the presence of adult worms, but does not discern them directly. A newer test finds a specific antigen produced in the presence of adult female heartworms. This test should be done yearly, before your dog starts the next season's medication. The best age to begin heartworm prevention, especially if you live in a region with a heavy mosquito infestation, is between 9 and 12 weeks. Your Cairn safely can take a once-a-month pill or chewable tablet, or a daily chewable. These may be used year-round or for the duration of mosquito season. Newly developed preventives also help to combat hookworms, roundworms, and whipworms.

Neutering: The most important step you can take to ensure your Cairn's health—next to obtaining yearly vaccinations—is to neuter your puppy before it reaches sexual maturity. The surgical procedure in which the sex organs are removed is called spaying in females and castrating in males. Neutering not only avoids the possibility that a dog will become accidentally pregnant or sire an unwanted litter, but also offers numerous benefits to its physical and emotional well-being. For example, spaying before six months of age nearly eliminates the chances that a female will contract mammary, uterine, or ovarian cancers. It also avoids the problems associated with twice-yearly heat cycles. The hormonal changes that take place during these seasons may be one of the risk factors for developing reproductive cancers.

Males, too, benefit from early castration. They are less likely to show undesirable behaviors, such as marking their territory or roaming. Castration also helps to reduce the possibility of developing testicular cancer, prostate disease, hormonal dysfunction, and perianal adenoma, a growth around the anus. Although neutering is major surgery, it's considered safe—especially for young dogs with immature reproductive organs. (Neutered dogs cannot compete in the show ring, but may participate in all Obedience and Performance events.)

Basic Procedures

Checking the pulse rate: To count your Cairn's heartbeat, place your hand directly over its heart, on the left side of the chest behind the elbow. You also can take the pulse at the femoral artery, located at the inner part of the thigh. In healthy dogs, the pulse is strong and steady. A normal rate may be up to 220 beats per minute in puppies, and 60 to 160 in adults. A rapid or slow pulse can signal different ailments, so always bring changes in the heart rate to the veterinarian's attention.

Collecting fecal and urine samples: If your dog is sick, you may need to collect fecal or urine samples to locate parasites or determine the cause of an infection. By viewing the samples under a microscope, the doctor is able to prescribe the best medication, as well as monitor the treatment process. If your pet has an infection or shows signs of kidney disease, you may need to collect samples throughout the course of the illness. To obtain a urine sample, place a small disposable container under your dog when it urinates. Then, transfer it to a clean bottle. Always collect urine in the morning when it's more concentrated. Fecal specimens should be examined within three hours of obtaining them, especially if the veterinarian must check for parasite eggs. When eggs mature and burst, they become more difficult to identify.

Giving medication: To give your dog a pill, grasp the top of its muzzle behind the canine teeth and gently press the lips inward until it opens its mouth. With your other hand, place the tablet as far back on the tongue as possible. Close your dog's mouth, tilt its head back, and stroke its throat until it swallows. If your pet has difficulty taking pills, place them in small treats. A small pill may be concealed in a bit of cheese, meat, or peanut butter and offered to the Cairn. If your dog is used to treats it will generally swallow the medication easily. Check to make sure the pill has not been rejected while the treat is swallowed. Some medications are specially coated, time-release formulas, so never crush a pill without checking with the doctor. To give liquid medicine, use a plastic eyedropper marked with a measuring scale. Form a pocket between your dog's cheek and teeth by gently pulling the skin outward. Hold

its head upright and slowly squeeze a small amount of liquid into the pocket. Stroke its throat until it swallows. Never pour liquids directly down the throat because your pet could choke or inhale the fluid.

Taking temperature: Lubricate a rectal thermometer with petroleum jelly and insert the bulb about an inch into your dog's rectum. Hold it in place for the recommended length of time, depending on the kind of thermometer you're using. A new thermometer is now available that is used in the ear and has a digital readout.

Normal body temperature is between 100.5° and 102.5°F. Slight variations may be due to excitement or exercise, but a reading higher than 102.5°F usually indicates a fever.

Advances in veterinary medicine, combined with research into the aging process, offer dogs the hope of optimal health and increased lifespans.

Common Ailments

Anal sac problems: Located on the lower left and right sides of the anus are two anal sacs. Although their exact purpose is unknown, the secretion they produce may lubricate the rectum and allow dogs to pass their bowel movements more easily. The distinctive scent from the sacs also might help animals determine the sex of others during greeting rituals. Sometimes the sacs don't empty fully and

Avoid taking your puppy to places where dogs gather until it's fully vaccinated at 16 to 20 weeks of age.

become impacted with material. When this happens, you may notice your Cairn is scooting across the floor or trying to lick the area. The veterinarian can express the fluid by gently pressing the sacs. If the sacs become infected, they can swell and rupture through the skin. These abscesses usually respond to antibiotics, warm compresses, and low doses of aspirin.

Constipation: Dogs normally have a bowel movement after each meal. However, if your pet routinely has fewer movements, it's no cause for concern. Dogs with constipation usually strain or feel pain when they attempt to have a movement. Constipation may occur if your Cairn eats a low-fiber dinner, or when it overeats. It also results from eating indigestible material, such as grass, paper, or cloth. Never give your dog natural bones because they can splinter and cause fecal impaction. For occasional bouts of constipation, give Milk of Magnesia or add a teaspoon of mineral oil to your dog's dinner. Change to a food with more fiber, and make certain your Cairn gets plenty of exercise. If constipation persists, contact the veterinarian.

Diarrhea: This is a common complaint in all breeds, partly due to the dog's short colon, which has difficulty absorbing all the fluid from undigested food in the intestines. Changes in diet, infections, worms, allergies, and stress also can cause diarrhea. For mild cases, withhold food for 12 to 24 hours, but provide ice cubes for water. Give one-half to one teaspoon of liquid antidiarrhea medication every four to six hours. Follow with a bland diet of lean hamburger, cottage cheese, cooked egg, or rice. If you notice vomiting, fever, or blood in the feces, or diarrhea lasts longer than 36 hours, consult the veterinarian.

Worms: Those that affect dogs include roundworms, tapeworms, hookworms, and whipworms. Dogs can acquire worms in the uterus or through nursing from an infected mother, or from contact with contaminated soil or feces. Worms also may enter the body as a result of eating raw meat or fish. Fleas play a role in the spread of tapeworms, serving as the intermediate hosts. Pets usually get worms by sniffing or licking infected material. However, the larval stage of hookworms can penetrate the skin.

Because puppies may be born with worms, their stools should be examined at two to three weeks of age and again at five to six weeks. Be sure to bring a fresh stool sample to the first veterinary appointment. To prescribe the best medication, if it's needed, the veterinarian must examine the specimen under a microscope to identify the kind of worm involved. He or she then can choose the safest product to use. When your pet is rid of worms, you can help to prevent reinfestation by keeping your yard clean and free of feces. Also, avoid places where strange dogs come together. Worms are less of a problem in adult dogs, because they seem to acquire some natural immunity that helps them fight off the parasites.

Vomiting: Cairns may vomit as a result of excitement, nervousness, motion sickness, worms, or overeating. Several serious diseases also may cause vomiting. If your dog vomits, but seems normal with no other signs of illness, the condition probably is not serious. Withhold food for 12 to 24 hours, but provide ice cubes for water. Feed a bland diet for a day or two, and allow plenty of rest. If your pet has a fever, diarrhea, vomits blood, indicates pain, or is sick for more than 24 hours, contact the veterinarian.

Health Problems

The Cairn Terrier is a hardy, vigorous, long-lived dog that usually remains active and playful from puppyhood through its distinguished senior years. In fact, a lifespan of 14 to 17 years is common. However, breeders, owners, and

The Cairn Terrier Open Registry accepts test results for the following hereditary diseases:
- ◆ Cataracts
- ◆ Entropion
- ◆ Progressive retinal atrophy
- ◆ Retinal dysplasia
- ◆ Corneal dystrophy
- ◆ Globoid cell leukodystrophy (Krabbe's disease)
- ◆ Hip dysplasia
- ◆ Legg-Calvé-Perthes disease
- ◆ Luxated patellas, elbows, and shoulders
- ◆ Craniomandibular osteopathy (lion jaw)

veterinarians have identified several health problems that are significant to anyone considering the addition of a Cairn to the household. Some of these are hereditary (passed from one generation to another through the genes) or congenital (present at birth). Others occur as a result of nonspecific factors, such as infections, exposure to environmental toxins, injuries, or advancing age. The Cairn Terrier Club of America and the Cairn Terrier Health Watch, in the United Kingdom, have conducted studies that have uncovered the presence of the conditions listed below. Since 1993, the CTCA and the Institute for Genetic Disease Control in Animals have maintained an open registry for Cairn Terriers. To help reduce the occurrence of hereditary diseases in their bloodlines, breeders voluntarily submit their dogs' test results for research purposes, as well as for use by individuals who seek to make sound breeding decisions.

Eye Problems

Cataracts: The loss of clarity of the lens of the eye, cataracts are one of the most common eye disorders among dogs. When light no longer can focus on the retina, located at the back of the eye, vision becomes cloudy or blurred. If the cataract continues to grow unchecked, the dog may lose its sight altogether. Because pets readily adapt to changes in vision, especially in familiar surroundings, owners may not notice the onset of cataracts until the veterinarian discovers them during a routine examination. The most successful way to treat cataracts is to surgically remove the lens. Although this results in reduced clarity, dogs can function around the house with only partial vision. Recently, veterinary ophthalmologists have begun to implant artificial lenses within the eyes, much like the procedure used in human cataract surgery.

Glaucoma: This is a serious disease that can cause pain, blindness, and even loss of the eye if not treated. Normally, the eye produces fluid that drains slowly from an opening at its front—the meeting point of the cornea and iris. Anything that interferes with this inflow or outflow results in a buildup of pressure within the eye. This prevents blood from reaching the retina, causing permanent damage to the optic nerve. Cairns have been found to have a specific form of the disease, called **pigmentary glaucoma,** in which the iris thickens and tiny spots of pigment develop and accumulate in the cornea. Eventually, the spots block the drainage passageways, causing pressure and nerve destruction. Another problem that can lead to glaucoma—especially in certain terrier breeds—is **lens luxation**. Located behind the iris, the lens is held in place by suspensory ligaments. When the fibers become weakened or break, the lens can slip from its normal position (subluxation) or become totally detached (luxation). Some forms of luxation block the outflow of fluid, while others cause damage to the cornea.

Signs of glaucoma, which usually appear after the disease has progressed, include teariness, abnormal discharge, reddened eyes, sensitivity to light, and pain reactions such as withdrawal or loss of appetite. Ultimately, the pupil may become fixed and dilated (large), and the eyeball may swell in size. Glaucoma leads to not only blindness but also pain, so prompt veterinary attention is essential. Although medication doesn't have the success rate in dogs that it does in humans, drugs that reduce inner eye pressure and keep the pupil relatively constricted help some animals with only partial lens luxation or mild glaucoma.

Another eye disease that affects Cairns—and more than 80 breeds worldwide—is **progressive retinal atrophy** (PRA). Transmitted as a recessive trait, meaning both parents must carry the defective gene (or genes), PRA refers to the degeneration of the photoreceptors located on the retina. These specialized cells, known as rods and cones, are responsible for vision in dim light and bright light, respectively. Usually, rods lose their functional ability before cones, leading to the classic symptom of night blindness. PRA affects both photoreceptors in Cairns, with the age of onset less than one year. The breed also is susceptible to a condition called **retinal dysplasia,** or the malformation of the retina.

Along with poor night vision and difficulty moving around in darkened rooms, another sign of PRA is the noticeable shininess of the eye. This is caused by the increased reflectivity of the tapetum behind the retina. Late in the disease, the lens may become cloudy or opaque and cataracts may form. Although there is no treatment for PRA, dogs rarely experience discomfort and usually adapt to their environments if given a little extra care by their owners.

An important resource for those interested in learning about hereditary eye diseases is the Canine Eye Registry Foundation (CERF) at Purdue University. (See Information, page 91.)

Neurological Disorders

Globoid cell leukodystrophy (GCL), or **Krabbe's Disease**, is a rare illness of the nervous system that infrequently occurs in Cairn puppies, as well as West Highland White Terriers and several other breeds. Beginning as early

Owners can help to make their pets more comfortable during their golden years.

between seizures, is believed to be inherited as a recessive trait, possibly involving two genes. Although the exact cause is unknown—and many factors may be responsible—epilepsy is thought to result from a chemical imbalance within the brain. Seizures take place due to the rapid, uncontrolled discharges of nerve cells. In Cairns, epilepsy usually begins by one or two years of age. Treatment, the success of which depends on the severity of the disease and its underlying causes (infection, tumor, cancer, head injuries), involves giving the antiseizure drug, phenobarbital, or a combination of medications.

Cardiovascular Disorders

Hemophilia A and **B** and **von Willebrand's Disease** (vWD), a group of blood clotting disorders, have been identified in a number of breeds. Transmitted as a sex-linked recessive trait, meaning the defective gene is carried by females but the disease appears mainly in males, hemophilia results from deficiencies in coagulation factors that allow the blood to clot properly. Von Willebrand's disease, which may be inherited from one or both parents depending on the form, comes from a decrease in a blood protein necessary for platelet function. Both cause abnormal bleeding, which first may be noticed during dewclaw removal or a routine surgical procedure. Other signs include unexplained bleeding from the nose or mouth, blood in the urine or feces, bruising, and swollen joints. Dogs with vWD often benefit from thyroid supplements. However, those with hemophilia may need occasional blood transfu-

as four weeks of age, GCL is a degenerative disease of the brain and spinal cord—and sometimes the peripheral nerves—that comes from a deficiency of a specific enzyme involved in lipid metabolism. Because GCL attacks the central nervous system, signs include weakness, loss of coordination, stumbling, tremor, blindness, and paralysis. There is no treatment for this recessively transmitted disease and affected puppies usually die by five or six months. A significant advance in eliminating GCL from bloodlines now exists with the development of a DNA-based blood test that can identify dogs that carry the defective gene.

The most common neurological problem, found in up to 5 percent of dogs, is the group of seizure disorders called **epilepsy.** Primary epilepsy, in which test results remain normal sions. Recent studies on the transmission of vWD have led to the first DNA tests to identify affected, carrier, and clear dogs. Several breeds now can be evaluated, including Scottish Terriers (a relative of the Cairn), from a swab of cells from inside the dog's cheek.

An uncommon problem of the cardiovascular system, usually found in puppies between 6 weeks and 12 months of age, is **portosystemic shunt**. Caused by a congenital defect that prevents the blood supply of the abdominal organs from reaching the liver, where toxins are removed, the disease mimics the signs of liver failure: abnormal behavior or seizures, lack of coordination, and overall poor health.

Skeletal Disorders

An abnormality of the lower jawbone that affects Cairns, Westies, and several other breeds is **craniomandibular osteopathy** (CMO), or "lion jaw." Seen in puppies less than one year of age, signs include pain during chewing and sensitivity when their mouths are handled.

Luxating patellas, or slipping kneecaps of the hind legs, are a common orthopedic problem in small dogs. Caused by weakness in the ligaments that support the kneecap, poor alignment of muscles and tendons, or a too-shallow groove in the femur, signs of patellar luxation include sudden limping, chronic lameness, or difficulty straightening the knee, usually accompanied by pain. Veterinarians can diagnose the disorder by manual examination of the kneecap, and by radiographs. Treatment involves rest, controlled exercise on leash, pain medication, and weight reduction, if needed.

The canine hip is a ball-and-socket joint in which the muscles and ligaments, as well as the shape and fit of the ball (femoral head) within the socket (acetabulum), maintain stability yet provide a full range of motion. **Hip dysplasia** (HD), mainly observed in large breeds, and **Legg-Calvé-Perthes disease** (LCPD), seen in small breeds, occur in Cairn Terriers. Dogs with HD are usually born with normal-looking hips that later undergo structural changes. Loose ligaments, inadequate muscle tone, and shallow sockets are significant factors in developing the problem. LCPD, on the other hand, results from an interruption in the blood supply to the head of the femur. When vital nutrients cannot reach the area, bone cells die and the ball becomes flattened and distorted. Signs of the disorders include lameness, gait abnormalities, muscle wasting, and pain.

For more information about skeletal disorders in dogs, contact the Orthopedic Foundation for Animals (OFA), a nonprofit registry organization founded in 1966. (See Information, page 91.)

Other Problems

Conditions with a strong hereditary basis that also are found in Cairns include **cleft palate,** in which the palate fails to fully fuse before birth; **cryptorchidism,** one or both testicles retained within the abdomen; **atopic dermatitis,** allergic skin diseases; **cystinuria,** excessive excretion of the amino acid, cystine, in the urine; **hypothyroidism,** abnormally low production of thyroid hormones; and **inguinal hernia,** protrusion of an organ or tissue through a break in the muscular wall that occurs where the rear leg joins the body.

HOW-TO: FIRST AID

First aid is an emergency procedure administered to save your Cairn's life and prevent additional injury. It should never take the place of prompt veterinary attention. In case of serious accident or illness, remain calm and give priority to life-threatening conditions. Begin artificial respiration or heart massage, if needed. Control profuse bleeding before you attend to minor injuries.

Artificial Respiration

A dog can stop breathing for many reasons. Food, fluid, or a piece of toy or bone may block its air passages. Shock, injury, heart failure, and asphyxiation also can cause difficulty breathing. This is always a life-threatening emergency. Animals can die within three to five minutes after the oxygen supply has stopped. Make certain your

Correct position for mouth-to-nose artificial respiration.

dog's air passages are clear before you treat other injuries.

Manual Artificial Respiration:

◆ Place your dog on its side, extending the head and neck to straighten the airway.
◆ Open the mouth and pull the tongue forward. Remove any matter inside the mouth.
◆ Place both hands on the side, between the shoulder blades and last rib.
◆ Press firmly for two to three seconds.
◆ Release the pressure for two to three seconds.
◆ Repeat until your dog breathes on its own.

Mouth-to-nose Artificial Respiration (if the chest has been injured):

◆ Pull your dog's tongue forward and close the mouth.
◆ Blow into the nostrils until the lungs expand.
◆ Remove your mouth so that air is expelled.
◆ Repeat until your dog breathes on its own.

Bleeding

Severe bleeding is an emergency that requires immediate action. Always control bleeding before you treat minor injuries.

Keep your dog quiet and apply a sterile gauze pad or clean cloth to the wound. Press firmly until the bleeding stops. If you need to use a second gauze pad, place it directly over the original dressing without removing the first bandage. If this fails to control the bleeding, make a tourniquet from strips of gauze or cloth. Wrap around the injured limb above the wound (between the wound and the heart) and tie a half-knot. Place a pencil on top of the loop and knot. Tighten carefully to stop bleeding. *Tourniquets must be used with extreme caution to avoid cutting off the circulation to the affected area.* Be sure to seek immediate veterinary assistance.

Choking

Symptoms of choking include gasping for breath, gagging, pawing at the mouth or throat, and salivation. If your dog is deprived of oxygen, it can lose consciousness and die within a few minutes. A procedure similar to the Heimlich maneuver used for humans is often successful in dislodging food or a foreign object blocking your dog's airway:

Heimlich-like Maneuver

◆ Open your dog's mouth and pull the tongue forward.

See if you can reach the obstruction with your fingers or forceps.

◆ Place your dog on its side.

◆ Using both hands, press the abdomen below the ribcage with a firm upward thrust.

◆ Repeat until your dog expels the foreign object, or you can extract it with forceps.

◆ Give artificial respiration if breathing has stopped, and contact the veterinarian.

Fractures

Dogs can break their legs when they jump from a high surface, slip on snow or ice, or run loose and get hit by a car. Signs of a fracture include limping, crying out in pain, swelling at the site, or exposed bone. First, treat for bleeding or shock; then, pad the limb with a temporary splint. Wrap gently with gauze or cloth strips. Place splints on the top and bottom of the fracture and tie in place. You may need to muzzle a dog that snaps as a reaction to pain. Seek prompt veterinary assistance.

Cardiac Arrest

Your dog's heart may stop beating as a result of injury, poisoning, electrical shock (chewing an appliance cord), or serious illness. If you cannot detect a heartbeat, begin heart massage at once. You also may need to provide artificial respiration.

Heart Massage

◆ Loosen your dog's collar and check the airway for obstruction.

◆ Lay your dog on its right side.

◆ Place the palms of both hands on the top and bottom of the chest. (For puppies, place the thumb on one side of the chest and the fingers on the other.)

◆ Push downward with the hand on top, using the bottom hand for support.

◆ Repeat compression six times, then wait five seconds. (For artificial respiration, give two to three breaths.)

◆ Continue heart massage until the heart begins to beat on its own, or you cannot detect a pulse. A dog can live only three to four minutes after its heart has stopped beating.

Heat Exhaustion and Heat Stroke

Dogs don't perspire through their pores the way people do. Because they release body heat mainly through panting, they are unable to tolerate prolonged exposure to heat. The most common causes of heat strokes are leaving a dog in a closed car, kenneling outdoors without enough shade or water, and exercising in hot weather. Puppies, elderly or overweight dogs, and those with chronic health problems are most susceptible to heat exhaustion or heat stroke. Symptoms include elevated body temperature, rapid heartbeat, staggering, dilated pupils, and pale gums. Cool your dog immediately with cold compresses or ice packs, or soak it in cool water. Monitor its body temperature to make certain it does not fall below normal.

Shock

Shock—when a dog's circulatory system is unable to supply enough oxygen to vital organs—may result from poisoning, injury, heat stroke, or severe illness. Watch for a weak and rapid heartbeat, labored breathing, pale gums, cool skin, and low body temperature. Keep your dog warm and quiet, be sure its air passages are clear, and attend to serious injuries and bleeding. Shock is a critical emergency that can lead to coma and death without quick action.

RESPONSIBLE BREEDING

Should You Breed?

As a creative endeavor that combines scientific principles with artistic vision, dog breeding appeals to people for a variety of reasons. Some have handled dogs from other kennels and want the challenge of finishing their own champion. Others imagine the ideal specimen and want to test their ability to produce it. Many seek recognition in the show ring, along with acclaim from their peers. A few perceive dog breeding as a profitable hobby. Newcomers often yearn for puppies as a way to bring a measure of immortality to their beloved pets.

Although the progression from owner to breeder comes naturally to those who enjoy the special friendship dogs provide, raising quality Cairn Terriers involves far more than simply producing puppies. There are already too many homeless dogs—even purebred animals—destined to lose their lives in animal shelters to undertake the demands of breeding without careful consideration of the consequences. Before you bring another litter into the world, to directly or indirectly add to the problem of pet overpopulation, evaluate your motives for breeding, and your ability to commit your resources, both time and money, to the maintenance and improvement of the breed.

Breeders should have a home for every single puppy before the breeding even takes place.

Your Cairn's Physical Condition

Several months before you plan a mating, have the veterinarian examine your Cairn for any illnesses or structural abnormalities that might interfere with breeding, whelping, or nursing puppies. Be sure to bring a fresh stool sample, so the technician can check for worms or their eggs. Medications that kill worms may harm developing fetuses, so it's vital to eliminate any parasites before your female becomes pregnant. Also, have the veterinarian test for the infectious disease, canine brucellosis. Spread through contact with the urine, vaginal discharge, or milk of infected animals, brucellosis results in miscarriages, stillbirths, abnormal sperm, and infertility in dogs. Antibiotics help to treat the infection, but you should eliminate any dog that tests positive for the disease from your breeding stock. People are susceptible to a form of brucellosis, as well, so be sure to maintain strict cleanliness when handling infected or unfamiliar dogs.

Because the dam transfers protective antibodies to her newborns by way of her milk supply, have the veterinarian administer any necessary vaccinations at least 30 days before the mating. Screening for hereditary diseases also is an important part of the prebreeding checkup. Common tests include eye examinations for progressive retinal atrophy, radiographs for hip dysplasia and luxating patellas, and blood coagulation tests for von Willebrand's disease.

(Contact the CTCA for additional information on hereditary diseases and suggested tests.)

Sufficient Financial Resources

If you think breeding your Cairn might be a profitable enterprise, consider some of the typical costs involved in raising and selling puppies. In addition to the examinations, vaccinations, and screening tests described above, you'll need to pay the stud fee in advance of the service, along with transportation to and from the stud's kennel. After the mating, your female will need further checkups to ensure her well-being and that of the unborn litter. Also, figure on premium dog food for the dam and her puppies, a whelping box and supplies, the AKC litter registration fee, advertising expenses, and examinations, vaccinations, and wormings for the puppies before they go to their new homes. If the dam experiences any problems during pregnancy or whelping, she may need a cesarean section or other emergency procedures. As you can see, breeders rarely come out ahead when they sell quality puppies. Most are fortunate to recoup a portion of their cost. They breed solely because they love the Cairn and desire to contribute to the improvement of the breed.

The Right Age

Although your female may conceive during her first estrous cycle, which occurs between five and eight months of age, it's important to wait until the second or third season to plan a mating. By two to three years, she is physically as well as emotionally ready for the duties of motherhood. Waiting not only allows time for certain breed faults to appear, but also permits the veterinarian to test for genetic diseases. She may have earned a Conformation or Obedience title,

as well. Although three years is the latest for a first pregnancy, Cairns are capable of whelping healthy puppies into their seventh or eighth year. If you plan to register the litter with the American Kennel Club, keep in mind that the dam must have been more than 8 months but less than 12 years at the time of the mating.

Finding Good Homes for the Puppies

Because breeders have difficulty placing puppies in quality homes—despite the Cairn's scarcity in many parts of the country—most wait until they have found dependable buyers before they plan a litter. Before you decide to breed your female, ask yourself whether you're willing to care for the puppies throughout their lifetimes. Will you stand behind your dogs with a written guarantee? Take back a dog if the owner is unable to keep it? Honestly represent your kennel's quality and reputation? Advise buyers of the breed's good and bad points—even when you desperately want to sell the puppy?

The bottom line: If you proceed with your breeding plans, will you be as conscientious as the breeder from whom you originally purchased your Cairn Terrier?

The Right Stud Dog

Before you attempt to locate a compatible stud dog, you must have a thorough understanding of your female's strengths and weaknesses. How closely does she conform to the standard? What are her best attributes? Does she exhibit (or carry) any serious flaws? What characteristics *must* an acceptable stud provide? A good stud should not only enhance your female's virtues, but also compensate for any faults. However, the traits that need improvement should be in a balanced rather than an exaggerated form in the prospective stud. For example, don't try to offset a large female by choosing a tiny male. Such a mating won't produce medium-sized puppies, but it will introduce a new set of undesirable genes just as difficult to eliminate.

Because both dogs contribute equal shares of genetic material to their young, don't expect an outstanding male to correct the problems of a poor-quality female, or vice versa. Ask your female's breeder for advice on the prospective parents before you plan a mating. He or she should be able to provide detailed information on your Cairn Terrier's background—including her parents and grandparents, brothers and sisters—and may help you find a male that will mesh nicely with the bloodline. If you did not buy from a reliable kennel, or are uncertain where your female came from, don't breed her! She may be an adorable pet, but most likely is not of breeding quality.

You can see many stud dogs when you attend a local dog show, regional specialty, or the national CTCA Specialty. (Pay particular attention to the Stud Dog Class, in which the judge evaluates the quality of the offspring rather than the stud, himself.) Publications such as the *CTCA Yearbook* and *Terrier Type* magazine also provide photographs, pedigrees, and kennel information on popular stud dogs. To narrow your choices, contact several owners to find out what titles their males have earned in Conformation or Obedience, what faults and health problems they carry, whether the owners have conducted screening tests and their results, and what types of puppies their studs have sired thus far in their careers. Reputable owners are

honest about their dogs' accomplishments, and will usually ask extensive questions about your female's background and suitability as a mate, as well as your plans for the litter.

When you have decided on the stud you want to use, contact his owner well before your female goes into estrus (heat) to make the arrangements. Be sure to find out the stud fee and whether the dog will be available when you need the service. Most owners require that both parties sign a contract before they perform the breeding. A typical contract includes the stud fee and when it's due, whether the owner will accept a puppy instead of the fee, who selects the puppy and at what age, and what happens if the female produces only one puppy or fails to conceive. Clarify any questions you might have before you sign the contract.

Deciding which dogs to bring together challenges even experienced breeders. Only when you know what you hope to realize from a particular mating, and how those results fit into your long-term plans, can you begin to produce Cairn Terriers that will influence the breed for generations to come.

The Estrous Cycle

The complex physical, emotional, and behavioral changes that attend the estrous cycle result from fluctuating levels of four hormones: estrogen and progesterone, produced in the ovaries, and follicle-stimulating hormone and luteinizing hormone, made in the pituitary gland. Cairn Terriers usually experience their first cycles between five and eight months of age, and come into estrus twice a year thereafter. The interval between cycles averages six months, but ranges from 100 to 400 days.

Proestrus

Extending from the appearance of blood-tinged discharge to the acceptance of the male, proestrus averages nine days in dogs. Pheromones—hormone-like chemicals that are detectable only to other dogs—are secreted in the urine and attract males. During this phase, though, the female spurns their advances by growling, nipping, or moving away. Other changes that occur during proestrus include swelling of the vulva, increased thirst and urination—usually in "marking" behavior—excitability, and restlessness.

To protect your furniture and carpets from the flow of blood, look for sanitary pads and "doggie pants" in your local pet supply store. An external spray is available that reduces the scent that brings males to your doorstep. Chlorophyll tablets may work in a similar fashion.

Summer puppies can enjoy being outdoors—and it's easier for you to house-train them.

Estrus

At puberty, fluid-filled sacs begin to form around several of the eggs in the ovaries. The follicles then enlarge and protrude until they resemble a cluster of grapes. Rising levels of follicle-stimulating hormone act on the ovaries to stimulate the output of estrogen. This, in turn, leads to the surge of luteinizing hormone that causes the mature follicles to rupture at ovulation.

During estrus, which also averages nine days, the vulva is still enlarged. The discharge has become thinner and clearer, and has changed in color from dark red to pale yellow. However, the main signals that identify estrus are behavioral. The female may begin to flirt with the male by turning her hindquarters toward him, lowering her back, raising her pelvic area, and flagging her tail to one side.

Most females conceive when bred 10 to 12 days after the onset of proestrus, or one to three days following the first acceptance of the male. Because incorrect timing is the main cause of infertility, you may want to have the veterinarian perform tests to determine the best time to breed. Vaginal smears discern changes in the lining of the vagina caused by rising levels of estrogen. Blood and urine tests detect increases in progesterone and luteinizing hormone, which play key roles in ovulation. These tests are particularly useful if you plan to inseminate artificially because behavioral cues (such as mounting by the male) are unavailable.

If you don't intend to breed your female during a particular cycle, be sure to keep her away from intact males. Confine her indoors and always supervise her when she goes outside. Males are experts at climbing fences and negotiating kennel runs. If you discover that an accidental mating has taken place, have the veterinarian give a hormone injection within 24 hours to keep the fertilized eggs from implanting in the uterus. Or, if you have no plans for future litters, have her spayed.

Investigate potential stud dogs well before you plan to breed your female. The male you bring into your bloodlines will have a significant effect on your kennel for generations to come.

Metestrus

Influenced by the hormone progesterone, this stage averages 10 weeks in dogs. Metestrus begins when the female refuses the male and no longer releases pheromones that attract him. Both the vaginal discharge and vulval swelling have diminished, and her actions are more sedate. If the mating was successful, changes will take place within your Cairn's body to prepare her for whelping, nursing, and raising her puppies. This also is the phase during which false pregnancy results if your female has not been spayed.

Anestrus

The resting stage averages 125 days, but ranges from four to nine months. The uterus and vulva have returned to normal, vaginal discharge has ceased, and the ovaries remain dormant until the start of the next cycle. Although most females experience estrus twice a year, some have only one annual cycle and a few have three.

Mating Procedure

Ovulation usually takes place on the second or third day of estrus, so plan the first mating two or three days after the female accepts the male's mounting behavior. Choose a quiet area away from outside distractions, and place a piece of old carpet or rubber matting on the floor to provide secure footing. Don't feed the dogs ahead of time, but take them outside separately to urinate just before mating. The female should encourage the stud's advances if the timing is correct. If she moves away or growls, wait until the following day and try again.

If you have an assistant on hand, have him or her steady the female while you help to position the male. Be patient and give plenty of praise, especially if the dogs are inexperienced. After the male penetrates and begins thrusting, contractions within the vagina enable his penis to become fully erect. The *bulbus glandis*, a gland at the base of the penis, enlarges to "tie" the dogs together. Because the male discharges semen slowly, the pair must remain joined until he deposits the last fraction of fluid. Once he has stopped thrusting, help him turn around to a more comfortable rear-to-rear position. Steady both dogs, so neither attempts to pull apart. *Never* forcibly break a tie. Doing so could injure one or both dogs. The union may last up to 30 minutes, but a lengthy tie is not required to ensure pregnancy.

After the male has finished ejaculating, the female's vaginal muscles relax so the pair can separate. Let her rest in her crate for several hours before you take her outside to urinate. This will help the semen remain in the vaginal tract, and increase the chances that she will conceive. Repeat the mating in 48 hours. Some breeders plan a third mating, as well, in case the timing was incorrect. Always keep the female securely confined until she goes out of season. During estrus, she will accept any other male and can be impregnated by him—in addition to the sire of choice. Puppies from such a mating are not eligible for AKC registration without further DNA testing to determine parentage, so take precautions!

Pregnancy

The gestation period, from conception to the onset of labor, averages nine weeks in dogs. To gauge when the puppies might arrive, count ahead 58 days from the first mating and 65 days from the second (if she was bred more than once). Mark the dates on your calendar, so you'll know when to begin watching for indications of impending birth. During the first month, it's difficult to tell whether or not the mating was successful. If your

Allow the dogs to become acquainted, under supervision, before the mating takes place.

female is young, or carrying only a single puppy, she may not show until the fourth or fifth week. Some owners have the veterinarian perform ultrasound or blood tests to detect pregnancy. By the second month, you'll notice that the developing puppies have started to form distinct round swellings within the uterine horns. You'll also see that her nipples have become enlarged and now look pink in color. During the last two to three weeks, you may be able to feel the puppies' kicks and movements if you gently place your hand over her abdomen. Be sure to give your Cairn plenty of love and tenderness during this stressful and often confusing period. Although some dogs prefer to remain by themselves, resting and sleeping undisturbed in their crates, others seek out the support of special family members.

Feeding and Exercise

For the first five to six weeks of pregnancy, your Cairn's energy requirements remain stable and she can continue to eat her regular maintenance diet. However, by the last few weeks, her nutritional needs have increased considerably, especially if she is carrying a large litter. To ensure that she is consuming enough protein, vitamins, and minerals to nourish her unborn puppies, switch to a high-quality growth formula—the same food you plan to feed the little ones when they are weaned. Because she may be unable to ingest all she needs in two meals, change to three or four smaller portions. Always provide plenty of fresh drinking water, as well.

Exercise is important during pregnancy. It not only assists in weight control, but also develops good muscle tone that aids in the whelping process. Schedule a brisk walk around the block once or twice a day, but avoid letting your Cairn play strenuously with other dogs. By the final weeks, change your pace to a leisurely stroll, but don't give up exercise entirely. Also, take care that she does not injure herself by jumping on or off furniture.

The Welcome Box

Several weeks before the anticipated due date, begin to prepare the whelping box. This is where the mother will welcome her brood into the world, and they will spend most of their time for the next few weeks. Well-made boxes are available from pet supply stores, or you can construct one of your own from a kit or specification sheet. The box should be large enough to allow the dam to lie down and stretch out without crowding her puppies. Look for a box about 20 inches (50 cm) high and 40 by 40 inches (100 cm × 100 cm) square. The puppies can't crawl over the sides, but the mother can come and go through the cut-out doorway. Make certain the box has a protective ledge around the inside walls to prevent the dam from accidentally crushing or smothering her puppies if she presses against the side of the box.

Because dogs prefer to whelp in privacy, install the box in a quiet area away from family activities. The dining room or a spare bedroom is ideal. (It's a good idea to introduce the dam to the whelping box a few weeks ahead of time, and permit her to sleep there if she seems interested.) To keep the puppies warm at all times, add a heating pad or temperature-controlled "nesting area" to the box. Line the bottom of the box with several layers of newspapers or blank sheets of newsprint. Avoid using color sections because they may contain harmful dyes. Include some clean towels or a bath mat, so the puppies will have good traction when they nurse and crawl around. Finally, outfit a small cardboard box with a hot water bottle and towels to hold the newborns while the dam is busy whelping the rest of the litter.

Whelping

The first signs of labor are behavioral. Your Cairn may seem more apprehensive and agitated than usual. She may change from one position to another, but have difficulty getting comfortable. Because the unborn puppies are pressing on her bladder, she may need to go outside more frequently. Her appetite may fall off a day or two before she delivers. Trembling, shivering, and panting occur when contractions begin. A key indication is the initiation of nesting behavior—shredding newspapers or collecting soft pieces of clothing for the whelping box. Some Cairns seek a quiet place to deliver their offspring, while others prefer to remain close to their owners.

Reassure your dog if she seems apprehensive. Speak in a soft

voice, and remain calm and comforting.

Contact the veterinarian a few days before the due date to find out who will be on duty for an emergency office visit or house call. Keep your telephone and important numbers near the whelping box. If you have arranged for an experienced breeder to aid in the delivery, be sure to inform him or her of any changes in your Cairn's condition.

Temperature Changes

Declining levels of progesterone in the bloodstream cause the body temperature to fall about 12 to 24 hours before the onset of labor. Take your Cairn's temperature, morning and evening, starting on the 57th day of gestation. When you notice a drop, from an average of 101.5°F (38°C) to 99° (37°C), or below, whelping will begin in a few hours. A test kit that measures progesterone levels in the bloodstream also helps to pinpoint the time of delivery.

Active Labor

If you have not already done so, carefully place your Cairn in the whelping box. As the contractions intensify, she may pant heavily, look anxiously at her flank, or try to lick her vulva. She may take a sitting position, bracing herself against the box, or lie on her side to deliver her young. Before the first puppy descends into the birth canal, a fluid-filled sac, or bubble, appears at the opening of the vulva. The sac ruptures spontaneously, or from the dam licking it, to provide additional lubrication. After a few more contrac-

The first clues of impending motherhood are often behavioral.

tions, the puppy arrives encased in its amniotic sac. If this is your Cairn's maternal debut, she may need your help in breaking the sac so the puppy can breathe. Hold the newborn with a dry towel and gently pull the membrane away from its head. Then, use a cloth or a bulb syringe to clear any remaining fluid from its nose and mouth. Let the mother take over licking and caring for her youngster. When the next set of contractions signals that another puppy is on the way, remove the newborn to the cardboard box that you have prepared ahead of time.

These irresistible six-week-olds will soon leave their littermates for new homes.

Tying the Umbilical Cord

When a puppy is born, it's still attached to the placenta by the umbilical cord. Although an experienced dam knows how to sever the cord by chewing it, you may need to help her if she fails to do so. To cut the cord, clamp the forceps about an inch or two from the puppy's belly. Trim the cord on the opposite side of the clamp, leaving the forceps in place until the bleeding stops. Tie the ends of the umbilical cord with unwaxed dental floss, dipped in rubbing alcohol. Cut the ends of the floss, so the dam can't pull on them and injure the puppy's navel. Dab the umbilical cord with iodine. As it dries, it will shrink and will fall off in a few days.

Passing the Placenta

A retained placenta can cause a serious uterine infection, so make certain the dam passes one for each puppy she delivers. Some females

Whelping Supplies

- Whelping box
- Heating pad or infrared lamp
- Clean newspapers and towels
- Scissors and Kelly forceps
- Unwaxed dental floss
- Iodine and other antiseptics
- Surgical gloves
- Lubricating jelly
- Scale for weighing puppies
- Nursing bottles and milk replacement formula

show an interest in consuming the placenta, which contains hormones that help the uterus to contract and that stimulate milk production. Permit her to have one or two, if she desires, but more than that may cause diarrhea or vomiting.

Postwhelping Care

After the dam has whelped the last of her puppies, gently cleanse her abdomen and hindquarters with a warm, wet washcloth. Take her outside for a brief walk around the backyard. By this time, she should be ready for a meal—either her growth-formula dog food, or light soup or broth. Remove the soiled newspapers from the whelping box and put down a fresh layer. As soon as she has eaten, return her puppies to her and be sure they are nursing properly. Schedule a visit with the veterinarian, and bring along the newborns for their first checkups. It's important to catch problems early, before the health of your Cairn Terrier or her puppies suffers. When the puppies are two or three days old, have the veterinarian remove their dewclaws.

Caring for the Puppies

First Meal

Be sure each puppy nurses freely of the dam's colostrum, or first milk, which contains antibodies and growth hormones. Although an adult dog's digestive tract breaks down these large molecules, newborns are able to fully absorb immunoglobulin during the first 24 to 36 hours after birth. This early intake of fluid also aids the cardiovascular system by increasing the volume of blood. Most puppies find the food source naturally, attracted by the dam's warmth and nudging. If one has difficulty, though, set it near a nipple and express a bit of milk onto its tongue. Hold the puppy in place a few moments until it begins to suck on its own. If the litter is large, or a puppy fails to grow and develop, you may need to supplement the dam's milk with a commercial "bitch's milk" replacement formula. It's a good idea to have nursing bottles and canned milk on hand before you anticipate needing them.

Environment

The first two weeks are critical to the puppies' survival. Because newborns cannot regulate their body temperature, make certain the room in which the whelping box is located is maintained at 85°F (29°C) during the first week, and 80°F (26°C) thereafter. Normally, the dam requires little assistance in feeding, cleaning, and caring for her brood. Born blind, deaf, and unable to walk, newborns spend most of their time sleeping—when they are not eating. They need their mother's help to urinate and defecate, and she keeps the whelping box clean and tidy, as well. Because puppies remain susceptible to infectious diseases despite receiving some immunity from their mother's milk, most breeders refrain from allowing visitors in the kennel until the youngsters have received their first inoculations.

Weaning

When their eyes have opened and they start to move around on their own—usually by three to four weeks—most puppies start to notice their mother's food dish. To encourage them to eat solid food, mix the dam's high-protein dinner with warm water to form thick gruel. Show the puppies the bowl, or dab a little food on their mouths. Allow them to nurse for two meals a day, in the beginning, but continue to increase the amount of solid food until they are fully weaned by six weeks.

Finding Good Homes

You can start to interview prospective buyers when the puppies are about six weeks old. However, they should remain with their mother and littermates until 8 to 12 weeks. Be sure to provide each buyer with the AKC registration form, pedigree, health certificate, puppy food, a favorite toy and blanket, and detailed instructions on how to care for the new youngster. Include membership information for the CTCA or a regional breed club, as well. Remind buyers that you're available to answer questions or concerns, or help with any problems the owners might encounter. It's difficult to watch the babies leave home, but try to remember the joy

Whelping Complications

◆ Bloody or dark green discharge before the birth of the first puppy.
◆ Active labor for more than 45 minutes without delivering a puppy.
◆ Labor stops before the dam delivers all the puppies.
◆ A puppy appears to be stuck in the birth canal.
◆ Signs that the dam is in pain, trembling, shivering, or near collapse.

Contact the veterinarian immediately if any of these signs of distress occur.

and excitement you experienced when you adopted your own little Cairn Terrier. Through your dedication to responsible breeding practices, you've now passed the torch to a new generation of fanciers.

Prepare the whelping box several weeks before the expected due date. Note the protective ledge around the inside walls of this well-constructed box.

ACTIVITIES FOR YOU AND YOUR CAIRN TERRIER

Showing Your Cairn Terrier

Since the first group of sportsmen gathered on a Chicago field in the spring of 1874 to compare their dogs' appearance rather than hunting ability, dog shows have grown steadily in popularity in the United States. Last year, for instance, more than 1.3 million dogs competed at over 3,200 all-breed and specialty events. Cairn Terriers, according to statistics, earned 124 of the nearly 20,000 championship titles awarded by the American Kennel Club.

Why have dog shows gained such acceptance with owners and handlers, as well as the public? Many view showing as a competitive activity in which the entire family can take part. Adults and children have an opportunity to make friends and learn new skills as they travel to show sites throughout the country—and even abroad. Some begin as a hobby, perhaps with family pets. However, as they develop a critical eye for their chosen breed, a few persist to become noteworthy breeders. These dedicated individuals continue exhibiting to highlight their kennels' achievements, compare the results of their breeding programs with those of other kennels, and allow fellow breeders to see dogs that might improve their own bloodlines.

If you have an attractive Cairn that conforms to the breed standard (pages 10–11) and has a flashy "Look at me!" attitude, and you think you might enjoy showing it off in the ring, the best way to start is by attending a local show where you can watch experienced handlers and dogs compete in breed classes, and the more advanced Group and Best in Show judging.

Sponsoring kennel clubs usually have information available on handling classes and match shows that are open to the public. Although "fun matches" don't award championship points, they provide an excellent arena for preparing your dog and practicing your handling techniques. Also, inquire about becoming a member of the club. By volunteering your talents behind the scenes—or front and center—you'll not only enjoy a greater bond with your pet, but also make friendships that could last a lifetime.

Conformation Classes

Cairn Terriers at least six months old, registered with the AKC, and free of disqualifying faults may enter one of six regular classes to

Cairns enjoy a day at the park as much as children do.

Anatomy of the Cairn Terrier:
1. *Muzzle*
2. *Nose*
3. *Eye*
4. *Skull*
5. *Ear*
6. *Withers*
7. *Back*
8. *Tail*
9. *Loin*
10. *Stifle*
11. *Hock*
12. *Pastern*
13. *Elbow*
14. *Feet*
15. *Forechest*
16. *Shoulder*

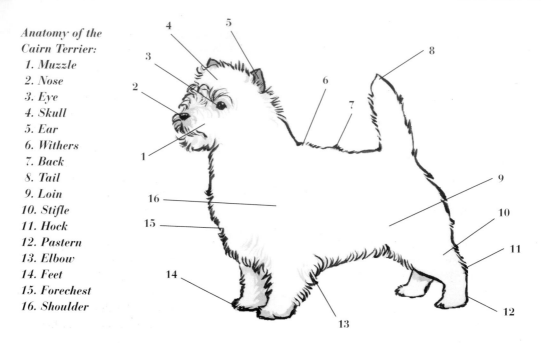

compete for their championships: Puppy, Twelve-to-Eighteen Month, Novice, Bred-by-Exhibitor, American-Bred, or Open. Each class is then divided into sections for dogs (males) and bitches (females). Because your Cairn may qualify for more than one class—Puppy and Novice, for example—always select the category in which it stands the best chance of finishing undefeated. (The six class winners are the only dogs that compete for points at a given show.)

Puppy Class: Puppies between 6 and 12 months compete in this class. Shows with a large number of entries, such as national or regional specialties, often further divide the field into Six-to-Nine Month and Nine-to-

Twelve Month Classes. The Puppy Class is ideal for youngsters that are not fully mature or lack experience in the show ring.

Twelve-to-Eighteen Month: Frequently held at large specialty shows, the Twelve-to-Eighteen Month Class recently gained AKC approval for inclusion at all-breed events, as well. This division, a stepping stone from Puppy to the more advanced classes, is open to all nonchampions between 12 and 18 months. Exhibitors and handlers often choose this class when they expect others to have many entries.

Novice: This class is for dogs that have not yet won three first prizes in Novice, a first place in Bred-by-Exhibitor, American-Bred, or Open, or one or more championship points.

The Novice Class often has fewer entries than the more popular Puppy and Open Classes, and it allows beginning handlers to compete with others at the same level.

Bred-by-Exhibitor: Dogs in this class must be owned or co-owned and handled by the breeder or an immediate family member. The Bred-by-Exhibitor Class is an excellent choice for breeders who seek to highlight their kennels' accomplishments.

American-Bred: When dog shows began in the United States, most of the victors came from established British and European bloodlines. To stimulate interest in domestic breeding programs, the AKC initiated a special class for American-bred dogs. Any dog (other than a champion) more than six months, bred and whelped in the United States, is eligible to compete in this category. Many exhibitors and handlers use American-Bred as a transition between Puppy and Open for immature or inexperienced dogs.

Open: Dogs more than six months, including foreign dogs, may compete in the Open Class. Professional handlers exhibit in this category, and dogs must be mature, properly trained and presented, and in top condition.

Winners: If your Cairn won a blue ribbon in its class, you'll return to the ring for the Winners Class. First, all the prizewinning males from the six classes compete for Winners Dog. This is the only male that receives points toward its championship at the show. The second-place male finisher earns the title Reserve Winners. Next, the female class winners meet to vie for Winners Bitch and Reserve Winners. (The second in the Winners Dog or Winners Bitch class is eligible for and *must* compete for Reserve.)

Best of Breed: After all the regular classes have been judged, the Winners Dog and Winners Bitch, champions of record, and dogs that have completed the requirements for their championships compete for Best of Breed. If your Cairn wins Best of Breed at an all-breed show, it may go on to the Terrier Group and, if it wins first place again, it then *must* compete with the six other group winners for Best in Show award. A dog that wins Best of Breed does not *have* to compete in its variety group. A dog that wins the group *must* compete for Best in Show.

Best of Winners: If the Winners Dog or Winners Bitch wins Best of Breed, he or she automatically receives the title Best of Winners. If another dog wins BOB, the two Winners compete against one another for Best of Winners.

Best of Opposite Sex: All entries of the opposite sex to the Best of Breed winner, including the Winners Dog or Winners Bitch, compete for the award Best of Opposite Sex. For example, if the BOB choice is male, all females in the class and the Winners Bitch compete for the BOS title.

Becoming a Champion

To become a champion, your Cairn must earn a total of 15 points. It must win six or more points at two shows—three or more points (called a major) at each show—from two different judges. An additional judge (or judges) must award the remaining points. An excellent specimen, therefore, can become a champion in three shows, by winning three five-point majors. The number of points your dog can win ranges from zero to five, depending on how many dogs it defeats. If the Winners Dog or Winners Bitch wins Best of Breed,

This dog eagerly awaits its turn in the ring.

for instance, all Best of Breed competitors are added to the number of defeated dogs to determine the points. If your dog wins the Terrier Group or Best in Show, it takes the highest number of points (usually five) earned in Group or Best in Show competition.

Ring Procedure

While you're waiting for your class to begin, watch the current exhibitors from ringside to determine the format of judging at that particular show. Although the procedure may vary

from show to show, depending on the size of the ring or its condition, weather, or the number of dogs competing, most judges follow the same pattern with each dog in the class. Typically, you and your dog will enter the ring in "catalog order," according to your armband number and listing in the show catalog. The entire group then gaits around the ring to give the judge a preliminary impression of the dogs' quality. Keep enough space between you and the other handlers so your dogs don't crowd one another. When your turn arrives for individual examination, carefully place your Cairn on the table. You may quickly tidy its coat, but avoid excessive grooming. A

The Cairn should look rough 'n' ready, rather than overly groomed.

Cairn should appear scruffy rather than highly stylized in the ring. The judge will inspect your dog's head and mouth, then proceed down its neck, front, shoulders, body, and hindquarters. If your dog is a male, the judge also will make certain that its testicles have fully descended in the scrotum.

Now your Cairn gets to show off! At the judge's direction, move your dog down and back on a loose lead. When you return to the starting position, your dog should stand at attention (called stacking) with no further handling. You may use a treat or squeaker to attract its attention. To complete your turn, take your Cairn around the ring, once again, to the end of the line of competitors. A judge might encourage a pair of terriers to "spar" in the ring to see how they react. The perfect "spar" is alert, intense, and beautiful—dogs at their natural best. There should *not* be growling, snarling, or snapping. This is not the intent of a spar! At the end of the judging, the first- through fourth-place winners receive their ribbons. When you receive any kind or color of ribbon from the judge it is polite and customary to say "Thank you." If your Cairn placed in its class, be sure to contact the show photographer to record your victory.

Obedience Competition

Before competitive Obedience began in the United States, most trainers directed their efforts toward the sporting breeds and working dogs. However, a well-known Standard Poodle breeder, Mrs. Helene Whitehouse Walker, sought to prove the intelligence and trainability of her dogs by devising a basic test that included off-leash heeling, retrieving a dumbbell, sit-stay and down-stay, recall, and broad jump. She also held the first all-breed Obedience test, in 1933, on her estate in upstate New York. Today, the American Kennel Club sponsors more than 2,200 Obedience trials, with over 100,000 dogs competing annually. Cairn Terriers have earned titles at all three levels—Novice, Open, and Utility—along with the coveted High in Trial and Obedience Trial Champion awards.

Any AKC-registered dog more than six months old is eligible to compete, including those with limited registrations. If you own an unregistered dog, such as an adopted or rescue dog, contact the AKC for an application for an Indefinite Listing Privilege (ILP) number. This allows your dog to enter all Obedience and Performance events. Neutered dogs and those with faults that would disqualify them in the show ring also may participate in these activities.

Getting Started

To learn more about Obedience, attend a local show where you can observe the dogs in the ring. Most kennel clubs offer basic instruction, and you also may find classes given by private trainers, humane organizations, veterinary clinics, or 4-H clubs. Ask to visit one of the classes without your dog. Is it well organized and efficiently run? Do the dogs enjoy working with their owners? Does the instructor clearly explain and demonstrate the exercises? How are the dogs disciplined and rewarded? Are you comfortable with the methods used?

Look for a trainer who has experience with terriers. Although Cairns are extremely intelligent—they are quick learners that figure out a particular task in the first few minutes of class—their independence and stubbornness often make them more difficult to work with than other breeds. "The key is to be as tenacious as they are," explains Lindy Sander, who has owned and trained several high-ranking Obedience Cairns, "and to find out what motivates the individual dog."

Keep in mind that you cannot force your will on a Cairn. "When a Cairn obeys, it's because the dog respects its handler," says veteran breeder Laura DeVincent. "Often, Cairns appear to have 'selective hearing,' and even the

Obedience training helps your dog develop into a good companion.

best-trained dogs may decide to take off if something more interesting comes along."

When training and competing with a Cairn, try to maintain a sense of humor and don't take their unexpected antics—in class or in the ring—too seriously. Few Cairns will achieve High in Trial, according to Betty Marcum, because they are too mischievous. "It's not that they cannot learn. They are highly intelligent, but just like to play tricks."

Scoring: Obedience exercises are rated on a point scale, based on the judge's mental picture of the ideal performance. "Willingness, enjoyment, and precision" on the part of the dog, and "naturalness, gentleness, and smoothness" in handling are key elements, state the AKC's *Regulations*. Each dog enters the ring with a perfect score of 200, and then loses points for mistakes like sitting crooked, failing to come when called, or retrieving an incorrect object. Errors in handling result in deductions, as well. Common problems include excessive leash corrections when heeling, using multiple commands, or physically assisting your dog. To earn a qualifying score, called a "leg" toward a title, your dog must achieve half of the required points in each exercise for a minimum of 170 points. After three qualifying scores, from three different judges, your dog receives its Obedience title.

There is no limit to the number of dogs that may qualify at a given show. All dogs that perform correctly earn their green qualifying ribbons and legs toward their titles. In addition, the four dogs with the highest scores in each

class receive ribbons and any special prizes offered by the show-giving club. The dog with the highest score, overall, earns High in Trial. If your Cairn qualifies or places in competition, be sure to have the photographer capture the win for your dog's photo album.

Novice: The beginning level, which grants the title Companion Dog (CD), consists of the basic commands that all dogs need to know to be good canine companions. Exercises include on- and off-leash heeling, standing in place for a physical examination by the judge, coming when called, and sitting and lying down for a predetermined length of time.

Open: The next level, which grants the title Companion Dog Excellent (CDX), is more difficult than Novice. Exercises include heeling off leash in different patterns, dropping to the down position during the recall, retrieving a dumbbell on the flat as well as over the high jump, leaping the broad jump, and sitting and lying down while the owner is out of the ring.

Utility: The most difficult level, which challenges even the brightest and most obedient

In Obedience, the Cairn must sit straight, and show willingness, enjoyment, and precision.

dogs—along with their handlers—grants the title Utility Dog (UD). Exercises include off-leash heeling with hand signals to stand, stay, drop, sit, and come, locating two articles by scent, standing for the judge's examination, and directed retrieving and jumping.

Special Awards: After your dog has earned its CDX and UD titles, it may continue to compete for the Utility Dog Excellent (UDX) award. Your dog must earn qualifying scores in both Open B and Utility B at 10 additional trials. (A minimum number of dogs, according to current AKC rules, must have competed in each class.) Dogs that have earned their UD titles also receive points when they place first or second in Open B or Utility B competition. To qualify as Obedience Trial Champion (OTCh), your dog must have won three first prizes (one each in

Dogs negotiate a series of obstacles, such as this tire jump, against the clock in Agility competition.

Open and Utility), from three different judges. It also must have accumulated 100 points, based on the number of dogs it defeated. The letters, OTCh, unlike most Obedience designations, precede your dog's official registered name.

Agility Trials

The sport of Agility originated 20 years ago at the renowned Crufts show in England. Based on the jumps and barriers of equestrian events, canine Agility proved so popular with spectators that The Kennel Club of Great Britain

granted it official status a year later. By the mid-1980s, trainers in the United States had discovered that Agility not only challenged their dogs to master a complicated series of obstacles, but also increased the connection they shared with their pets as both learned a new set of skills. Since its initiation by the American Kennel Club, in 1994, Cairn Terriers have gained titles in all three levels of Agility.

Certain aspects of Agility may favor larger dogs, but jump heights and course times are adjusted to give all breeds an equal footing. Because Cairns are vigorous and sturdy little terriers, they excel at jumping (most jump in the 12-inch division) and, of course, going through tunnels. They have an advantage on the narrow dogwalk, which consists of an up ramp and a down ramp connected by boards, and usually hit

Activities that require hunting and digging are all in a day's work for the Cairn.

the obstacles' required "contact zones." However, a trainer who has considerable experience working with small dogs, Gerianne Darnell, has found that some have difficulty scaling the six-foot-three-inch-tall USDAA A-frame. Others are confused by the weave poles—they are set too far apart for the dogs to visualize the pattern of going in and out. Small breeds also can lose valuable seconds waiting for the seesaw to come down, and a wet chute may be nearly impossible to penetrate on a rainy day, she says.

As with other forms of obedience, endless repetition bores the Cairn. Always maintain a positive attitude, and keep sessions interesting by using treats, play sessions, or other motivators, advises trainer Diane Eatherton. "The bottom line in agility is to have fun," she adds. "The titles really don't mean much if you don't have a happy and willing dog."

Scoring: To achieve a qualifying score, your dog must negotiate the course with speed and accuracy. Jumps may consist of single, double, and triple bar jumps; panel, window, and tire jumps; and the broad jump. Obstacles may include the dog walk, A-frame, seesaw, tunnels, weave poles, and pause table. The judge adds fault points to your dog's score for a variety of penalties: exceeding the course time, refusing an obstacle, crossing incorrectly, or not stepping on the contact zone. Although you may direct your dog with verbal commands and/or hand signals, you may not touch or physically assist it in any way. To receive an Agility title, your dog must execute three qualifying runs, under at least two different judges.

Titles: The AKC awards the titles Novice Agility (NA), Open Agility (OA), and Agility Excellent (AX). To receive the top-level Master Agility Excellent (MX) title, your dog must first acquire the AX title and then go on to earn qualifying scores at 10 additional trials.

Earthdog Tests

Designed for small terriers and Dachshunds, noncompetitive Earthdog tests assess your Cairn's instinctive and trained hunting and working abilities. The manmade "dens" consist of nine-inch-square liners set into trenches in the ground and covered with brush and other materials to look as natural as possible. At the end of the tunnel, which is scented like an actual den, is a securely caged pair of adult rats or artificial quarry. The object of the test is to follow the correct scent line, then "work" the quarry by barking, growling, digging, scratching, or lunging to show interest. Many Cairns, though, are "silent workers," according to Joyce Moore, an AKC-licensed Earthdog judge who also trains her Cairns for Earthdog events. "Barking is not always heard from the tunnel when the dog reaches the rat. Cairns are more inclined to dig, scratch, bite at the bars, and whine, which nonetheless constitute work from a judging standpoint. Getting to the quarry and staring at it *does not* qualify as work." Also, when dropped at the start of the test, "Cairns don't charge the tunnel, but are more apt to follow the scent trail and check out the entrance before going in," she adds. "Once in the tunnel, though, they are very fast in negotiating the turns and obstacles to reach the quarry."

The key to preparing for Earthdog trials is to begin when your Cairn is a puppy, with practice "hunting" sessions in the backyard. Moore suggests using a straight piece of PVC pipe, about 10 feet long, to accustom the puppy to entering and traversing a dark, narrow space with confidence. "Its favorite toy should await it at the other end," she explains, "as you tease it into a sense of accomplishment over finding the 'quarry,' and putting up a 'good old terrier tug' to 'shake its timbers.' The puppy will begin to revel in this game, displaying its natural instincts and the heart and soul of why it was bred to be here." However, never overtrain your Cairn or it will become bored and refuse to participate. Also, never force your dog into the tunnel, admonishes Moore. "This has to be a fun activity that allows it to exercise those instincts that were bred in many, many years ago."

Scoring: The basic test, Introduction to Quarry, is for novice dogs that have had no prior exposure to tunnel work. Entering a simple 10-foot passageway with a 90-degree turn, your dog must locate and then work the quarry for the specified length of time. The Junior Earthdog test is similar to the first test, but the tunnel is longer and contains three 90-degree angles. In the Senior Earthdog test, your dog must locate the quarry in a more complex den, with a scented false den and exit. In addition to correctly locating and working the quarry, your dog must leave the den on command. The most difficult test, Master Earthdog, is designed to simulate an authentic hunting situation. Your dog must distinguish the correct entrance from an unscented false passage, reach the quarry through a tunnel that consists of an obstacle and a constriction, and work the quarry as required. Dogs perform this test in pairs, with one dog staked near the entrance while the other works the quarry. After finishing in the den, the first dog changes places with the waiting dog. Dogs must qualify twice for the JE title, three times for the SE title, and four times for the ME title, from at least two different judges.

Titles: Dogs begin with the noncredit Introduction to Quarry, and then progress to Junior Earthdog (JE), Senior Earthdog (SE), and Master Earthdog (ME).

Tracking Tests

Developed in the 1930s as a component of the Utility Dog test, tracking measures a dog's ability to recognize and follow the scent of a human track layer. To navigate the terrain, which may include vegetation, gravel, sand, concrete, or other surfaces, your dog must work in a tracking harness on a 20- to 40-foot leash. You may give verbal commands and encouragement, but signals or movements that guide your dog to a particular location are prohibited. The AKC calls Tracking "a team sport in the truest sense." Fay Fowler Gross, who began teaching her Cairns to track in the early 1970s, agrees: "In every other area of training, the handler basically runs the show. This cannot be done in Tracking. Here, success means putting your faith in your dog to make the correct decisions. If you have gotten your point across to your dog that the scent at the starting flag is the one to pursue, all you have to do is follow along behind."

Close to Ground

Cairns, whose scenting ability rivals that of any working dog, do very well in Tracking, according to Gross. "A short-legged breed like the Cairn is already close to the ground, so it

Use a glove with your scent to train your Cairn in tracking.

Earthdog tests are designed to simulate authentic hunting situations. To pass the progressively more difficult tests, terriers must locate and work their quarry in "dens" of increasing complexity.

can investigate areas where larger dogs can't go. Its coat allows it to penetrate dense brush, as it protects it from harsh weather conditions. Cairns are agile and can climb almost as well as a cat. Many love to swim, too, so crossing water is rarely a problem."

To begin training, suggests Gross, place your dog in a harness with the leash attached. With another handler holding your dog, play with it to build enthusiasm. Then, quickly run out of sight and hide. The handler gradually lets out the leash, while giving the command, "Track!" or "Find it!" Remain hidden until your dog finds you, and praise it profusely when it succeeds. "Although many dogs begin looking and air scenting, they quickly put their noses to the ground and actually track where their owners have walked," says Gross. Searching for a favorite person or article is the best way to keep the dogs interested. "So many people think they have to do regulation tracks all the time," she adds. "I do them only occasionally. Remember, we are not teaching the dog a thing

The A-frame may pose difficulty for some small dogs, but not this athletic Cairn performing at a Scottish Highland Festival in Colorado.

A tunnel is formed by assembling nine-inch-square wooden liners. This Cairn is being lifted from the den at the end of its test.

This nine-week-old has mastered the basics of navigating a tunnel.

it does not already know—the handlers are the ones who need to learn to follow their dogs."

Scoring: To pass this test, your dog must follow the scent of the track layer and locate the article, or articles, he or she dropped. The article(s) must be presented to the judge at the end of the test. There is no time limit for finding the article(s), but your dog must appear to be actively searching. It earns its title by successfully completing one track.

Titles: AKC titles include Tracking Dog (TD), Tracking Dog Excellent (TDX), and Variable Surface Tracking (VST). To receive the title Champion Tracker (CT), your dog must earn all three tracking awards. The letters, CT, precede your dog's official registered name.

To learn more about dog shows, Obedience competition, Performance events, and other activities you can share with your Cairn Terrier, contact the American Kennel Club, your local kennel or training club, or the Cairn Terrier Club of America (see Information, page 90).

Kennel Clubs

American Kennel Club
260 Madison Avenue
New York, NY 10016
http://www.akc.org

Canadian Kennel Club
89 Skyway Avenue, #100
Etobicoke, Ontario, Canada
M9W 6R4

The Kennel Club
1 - 5 Clarges Street
Piccadilly, London, England
W1Y 8AB
http://the-kennel-club.org.uk

United Kennel Club, Inc.
100 East Kilgore Road
Kalamazoo, MI 49001
http://www.ukcdogs.com

Cairn Terrier Club of America,
   Inc.*
Mrs. Christine M. Bowlus
8096 Chilson Road
Pinckney, MI 48169
http://www.cairnterrier.org

The Foundation of the Cairn
   Terrier Club of America, Inc.*
David Wright, Finance Officer
804 Kent Circle
Bartlett, IL 60103

Cairn Terrier Club of Canada*
2706 Decew Road, RR #1
Fonthill, Ontario, Canada
L0S 1E0

The Cairn Terrier Club*
Mr. J. Berrecloth
6 Duff Street
Dundee, Scotland DD4 7AN

*This address may change when new
officers are elected. Current address may
be obtained from the American Kennel
Club or the Canadian Kennel Club.

The Cairn Terrier Association*
Mr. D. Compson
"Thistleclose," Six Ashes Road
Bobbington, W. Midlands,
England DY7 5EA

Southern Cairn Terrier Club (UK)
Cairn Terrier Health Watch
Mrs. Ruth Wadman Taylor,
   M.R.C.V.S.
E-mail: ruth-vet@manserv.co.uk
http://www.users.dircon.co.uk/~m
anserv/health.html

Cairn Terrier Books

*Cairn Terrier Champions:
   1952–1986.* San Francisco, CA:
   Camino Book Co., 1987.
Carter, Christine. *The Cairn
   Terrier.* Neptune City, NJ: T.F.H.
   Publications, Inc., 1995.
Cooke, Ryan and Cynthia. *The
   Cairn Terrier in Canada, Vol. 1:
   A Compilation of Canadian
   Cairn Terrier Records
   1920–1995.* Canada, 1997.
Marcum, Betty E. *The New Cairn
   Terrier.* New York, NY: Howell
   Book House, Inc., 1995.
McCormack, Erliss. *Cairn Terriers.*
   Neptune City, NJ: T.F.H. Publi-
   cations, Inc., 1995.
Vaughn, Clarence F. and David
   Fee. *The Cairn Terrier in Amer-
   ica.* Scottsdale, AZ: Privately
   published, 1994.

Antique; Out of Print; Hard to Find Books

Ash, Edward C. *Dogs: Their
   History and Development.*
   London: Ernest Benn Limited,
   1927.
Beynon, J. W. H. *The Cairn Terrier.*
   New York, NY: Arco Publishing,
   Inc., 1974.
Gordon, John. *All About the Cairn
   Terrier.* New York, NY: Viking
   Press, 1988.

Hutchinson, Walter, editor. *Hutchin-
   son's Dog Encyclopedia.* London:
   Hutchinson & Co., c. 1935.
Jacobi, Girard A. *Your Cairn
   Terrier.* Fairfax, VA: Denlinger's
   Publishers, Ltd., 1976.
Leighton, Robert. *The New Book of
   the Dog.* London, England: Cas-
   sell and Company, Ltd., 1912.
Marvin, John T. *The New Complete
   Cairn Terrier.* New York, NY:
   Howell Book House, Inc., 1987.
Rogers, Mrs. Byron. *Cairn and
   Sealyham Terriers.* New York,
   NY: Robert M. McBride &
   Company, 1922.
Ross, Florence M. *The Cairn Ter-
   rier.* Manchester, England: "Our
   Dogs" Publishing Company
   Limited, 1926.
Whitehead, Hector F. *Cairn Terri-
   ers.* New York, NY: Arco Pub-
   lishing, Inc., 1976.

General Dog Books

American Kennel Club. *The Com-
   plete Dog Book.* New York, NY:
   Howell Book House, Inc., 1998.
Carlson, Delbert G., D.V.M. and
   James M. Giffin, M.D. *Dog
   Owner's Home Veterinary
   Handbook.* New York, NY:
   Howell Book House, Inc., 1992.
Donovan, John A. K., William W.
   Denlinger, and R. Annabel
   Rathman. *Gaelic Names for
   Celtic Dogs.* Loveland, CO:
   Alpine Publications, Inc., 1996.
Kalstone, Shirlee and Walter
   McNamara. *First Aid For Dogs.*
   New York, NY: Arco Publishing,
   Inc., 1980.
Lehman, Patricia F. *Your Healthy
   Puppy.* Neptune City, NJ: T.F.H.
   Publications, Inc., 1998.
Lewis, Lon D., D.V.M., Ph.D., et al.
   *Small Animal Clinical Nutrition
   III.* Topeka, KS: Mark Morris
   Associates, 1987.

Migliorini, Mario. *Dig In! Earth-dog Training Made Easy.* New York, NY: Howell Book House, Inc., 1997.

Pinney, Chris C., D.V.M. *Caring for Your Older Dog.* Hauppauge, NY: Barron's Educational Series, Inc., 1995.

Rice, Dan, D.V.M. *The Complete Book of Dog Breeding.* Hauppauge, NY: Barron's Educational Series, Inc., 1996.

Streitferdt, Dr. Uwe. *Healthy Dog, Happy Dog: A Complete Guide to Dog Diseases and Their Treatments.* Hauppauge, NY: Barron's Educational Series, Inc., 1994.

Walkowicz, Chris and Bonnie Wilcox, D.V.M. *Successful Dog Breeding, The Complete Handbook of Canine Midwifery.* New York, NY: Prentice Hall Press, 1985.

Publications available from the Cairn Terrier Club of America
Cairn Terrier Grooming, Start to Finish
Clarification and Amplification of the Standard
Visualization of the Cairn Standard
The Cairn Terrier, by Baroness Burton
Meet the Cairn Terrier
CTCA Yearbooks 1978–1992

Dog Magazines
AKC Gazette
American Kennel Club
260 Madison Avenue, 19th Floor
New York, NY 10016

Bloodlines
United Kennel Club, Inc.
100 East Kilgore Road
Kalamazoo, MI 49001

Dog Fancy
Fancy Publications, Inc.
P. O. Box 6050
Mission Viejo, CA 92690
http://www.dogfancy.com

Dog World
PJS Publications, Inc.
29 North Wacker Drive
Chicago, IL 60606
http://www.dogworldmag.com

Dogs In Canada
43 Railside Road
Don Mills, Ontario, Canada
M3A 3L9
http://www.dogs-in-canada.com

Purebred Dogs in Review
P.O. Box 30430
Santa Barbara, CA 93130
http://www.dogrevu.com

Dogs USA
Fancy Publications, Inc.
3 Burroughs Drive
Irvine, CA 92718

PetLife
Magnolia Media Group
1227 West Magnolia Avenue
Fort Worth, TX 76104

Videos
Cairn Terrier
American Kennel Club
Video Fulfillment Department
5580 Centerview Drive, Suite 200
Raleigh, NC 27606

Movement in the Cairn
Cairn Terrier Club of America
Mrs. Christine M. Bowlus
8096 Chilson Road
Pinckney, MI 48169
http://www.cairnterrier.org

Organizations and Suppliers
American Boarding Kennels Association
4575 Galley Road, Suite 400A
Colorado Springs, CO 80915
http://abka.com

American Working Terrier Association
Membership, Cindy Todd
6861 Greenleaf Drive North
Richland Hills, TX 76180

Canine Eye Registry Foundation (CERF)
SCC-A Purdue University
West Lafayette, IN 47907

Institute for Genetic Disease Control in Animals
P. O. Box 222
Davis, CA 95617

Pet Sitters International
418 East King Street
King, NC 27021
http://www.petsit.com/index.html

The Orthopedic Foundation for Animals, Inc.
2300 E. Nifong Boulevard
Columbia, MO 65201-3856

United States Dog Agility Association
P. O. Box 850955
Richardson, TX 75085

I N D E X

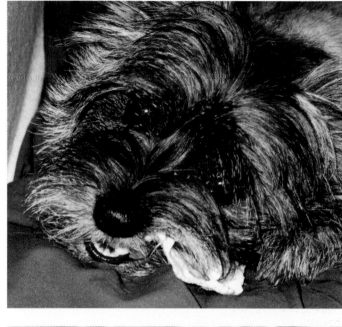

The Author

The author would like to express her appreciation to the following contributors: Barbara Cole, Gerianne Darnell, Laura De Vincent, Diane Eatherton, Fay Fowler Gross, Louise Hooper, Betty E. Marcum, Joyce Moore, Lindy Sander, Sandra Speicher, and Natalie H. Winslow.

Photo Credits

Judith E. Strom: pages 4, 9, 14, 25, 27, 30, 35, 76, 91 top, bottom; Raphael Tuck and Sons: page 6; Kent and Donna Dannen: pages 10, 12, 22, 38, 52, 55, 89; Duff Munson: page 11; Laura De Vincent: pages 18, 36; Paulette Braun: pages 20, 64; Lindy Sander: pages 26, 37, 56, 82; Donna J. Coss: page 42; Toni Tucker: pages 2–3, 46; Sandra Speicher: page 60; Sally Richerson: page 88.

Cover Photos

Donna J. Coss: front cover, back cover; Kent and Donna Dannen: inside front, inside back.

Important Note

This pet owner's guide tells the reader how to buy and care for a Cairn Terrier. The author and the publisher consider it important to point out that the advice given in the book is meant primarily for normally developed puppies from a good breeder—that is, dogs of excellent physical health and good temperament.

Anyone who adopts a fully grown dog should be aware that the animal has already formed its basic impressions of human beings. The new owner should watch the animal carefully, including its behavior toward humans, and should meet the previous owner. If the dog comes from a shelter, it may be possible to get some information on the dog's background and peculiarities there. There are dogs that for whatever reason behave in an unnatural manner or may even bite. Under no circumstances should a known "biter" or an otherwise ill-tempered dog be adopted or purchased as a pet or show prospect.

Caution is further advised in the association of children with dogs, in meeting with other dogs, and in exercising the dog without a leash.

Even well-behaved and carefully supervised dogs sometimes do damage to someone else's property or cause accidents. It is therefore in the owner's interest to be adequately insured against such eventualities, and we strongly urge all dog owners to purchase a liability policy that covers their dog.

Acknowledgments

Working as a freelance writer for more than 12 years, Patricia F. Lehman specializes in the topic of dogs and their care. Her articles and photographs have appeared in a variety of canine magazines, newspapers, and newsletters. Her books include *The Miniature Pinscher: King of Toys* and *Your Healthy Puppy*. She is a member, and former treasurer, of the Dog Writers' Association of America. Currently, she serves as treasurer of the Dog Writers' Educational Trust, an organization that grants scholarship funds to students with a background in dogs.

All inquiries should be addressed to:
Barron's Educational Series, Inc.
250 Wireless Boulevard
Hauppauge, NY 11788

http://www.barronseduc.com

Library of Congress Catalog Card No. 98-46011

International Standard Book No. 0-7641-0638-4

Library of Congress Cataloging-in-Publicaton Data
Lehman, Patricia F., 1955–
    Cairn terriers / Patricia Lehman; illustrated by Pam Tanzey.
        p.   cm. — (Complete pet owner's manual)
        Includes bibliographical references (p. 90) and index.
        ISBN 0-7641-0638-4
        1. Cairn terrier. I. Title. II. Series.
SF429.C3L44   1999
636.755—dc21   98-46011
                                CIP

Printed in China

P lucky little Cairn Terriers were originally bred in Scotland 400 years ago to assist their masters in routing foxes, badgers, otters,and other small "varmints" from their hidden dens. Their name derives from the Scottish *cairns*, or rock piles, that marked graves and property boundaries throughout the countryside. Today, their compact size, feisty but sweet temperament, and alert intelligence make these terriers popular with an ever-growing number of families. Happiest when working, the little busy-bodies are intrepid competitors at earthdog and obedience trials, tracking events, and conformation shows, where their "look at me" attitude wins hearts and ribbons.